DECISIONTIME

COMMITMENT COUNSELING

Arthur H. Criscoe, Leonard Sanderson

LifeWay Press
Nashville, Tennessee 37234

© Copyright 1987, 1998 LifeWay Press

Revised 1998

By Yvonne Burrage, Brian Daniel, and Henry Webb

Third Reprint • April 2003

ISBN 0-7673-9179-9

Dewey Decimal Classification: 253.5

This book is the text for course CG-0078 in the subject area Evangelism in the Christian Growth Study Plan

Unless indicated otherwise, Scripture quotations are from The Holy Bible, *New International Version,* copyright © 1973, 1978, 1984 by International Bible Society. Used by permission.

To order additional copies of this resource: WRITE LifeWay Church Resources Customer Service; One LifeWay Plaza; Nashville, TN 37234-0113; FAX order to (615) 251-5933; PHONE (800) 458-2772; EMAIL to *customerservice@lifeway.com;* ORDER ONLINE at *www.lifeway.com;* or VISIT the LifeWay Christian Store serving you.

Printed in the United States of America

Leadership and Adult Publishing

LifeWay Church Resources

One LifeWay Plaza

Nashville, Tennessee 37234-0175

Table of Contents

Week 1

Commitment Counseling

This week you will begin to understand the role of a decision counselor in the church. By the end of the week you should be familiar with the skills needed for decision counseling and how best to apply these skills.

Day 1:
What Is a Commitment Counseling Ministry?

Though commitment counseling is often a "behind-the-scenes" activity, it is a significant and rewarding ministry as you participate with God in leading others to follow His will. Christians are never happier than when they see other people become Christians. Second only to that is the joy of seeing Christians make deeper and more meaningful commitments as Christians. In short, invitation time is a time for rejoicing in your church.

What has impressed you most about Billy Graham crusades? Perhaps you remember most the invitation time when hundreds of people flooded the stadium aisles going forward to make new commitments to Christ. You are probably aware that many others were walking forward to serve as counselors for those making decisions.

People are especially thrilled when an evangelistic harvest occurs in their own church. There is not a more vital ministry than one that meets the needs of those who make public commitments of their lives to Jesus Christ. In many churches half or more of those who make a commitment to Jesus and to church membership will drop out. This decision counseling ministry is one strategy to reduce that significantly.

Later this week, you will be asked to make a commitment to training for a ministry of decision counseling by preparing for, attending, and participating in each session of the course. Pause for a moment and ask God to reveal clearly to you His will concerning your involvement in this ministry. Agree now to obey His leadership.

DecisionTime requires commitment. Because kingdom work is a responsibility to be taken seriously, this resource will require a faithful study each day. In addition to the daily work, there are weekly small-group sessions too. These sessions will give you an opportunity to share with other persons led to be decision counselors. This resource will use "commitment counseling/counselors" and "decision counseling/counselors" interchangeably.

The Need for Decision Counselors

Because ministry is everyone's responsibility, members can help pastors and other church staff meet the critical needs of the church. One of those needs is counseling new believers, persons desiring to become church members, and others making spiritual decisions.

The trained counselors may also serve the community of believers during area crusades, evangelistic rallies, youth and children's camps, evangelism conferences, or any other time public invitations are given.

Every church needs a group of dedicated and trained decision counselors for these reasons:
- To make sure the decision maker trusts Jesus.
- To clarify the decision being made.
- To encourage those making decisions.
- To help when several persons respond to the invitation.
- To maintain accurate records for follow-up.

The Counseling Team

The work of the church is the responsibility of all members. The entire church family can be a vital part of the commitment counseling ministry through prayer and encouragement. The involvement of church members is important in all aspects of decision counseling. The decision counseling team has seven functions. In the descriptions below you will see that two people can handle every function except decision counselor in some churches.

The Pastor

The pastor is the key person on the team. Without his support, the ministry will be weak, if it functions at all. He helps establish the commitment counseling ministry in a church. He will interpret the process for the church. In doing so, the church will understand the procedures for receiving those who make commitments during the invitation. The pastor helps to select decision counselors and also provides guidance for the entire decision counseling process. In many churches the pastor will also serve as the trainer, the receiver, and/or the presenter.

Coordinator

The coordinator provides practical supervision for the decision counseling ministry. The coordinator and the pastor may choose to set up a schedule of assigned services for the counselors. The coordinator works with the pastor to enlist decision counselors. He will also determine how many counselors are needed for each service. The coordinator is responsible for the decision counseling room. The coordinator might serve as trainer and/or advisor.

Trainer

The trainer or facilitator uses *DecisionTime: Commitment Counseling* to lead the training sessions that prepare decision counselors. The pastor or coordinator may also serve as the trainer.

Receiver

The receiver, generally the pastor, will stand in the receiving area during the invitation portion of a service. The receiver greets a person coming forward to make a decision, listens as the decision is being described, voices a brief prayer, and then introduces the person to a decision counselor. In larger churches, camps, or rallies there are often several receivers across the front of the worship center.

Advisor

The advisor is the most skilled decision counselor and needs to be prepared for any counseling need. The advisor is usually stationed in the counseling room or counseling area to assist counselors and decision makers. In some churches the coordinator will double as the advisor.

After the decision has been made, the advisor is available to assist with the distribution of follow-up materials and explain the presentation procedures. Some occasions may require more than one advisor.

Once commitment counseling is completed, the advisor is introduced to the decision maker and hears the person's decision. This serves two purposes. First, this gives the decision maker a chance to solidly affirm his decision. Second, if there is some doubt or question about the decision, the advisor can recommend further counseling.

Decision Counselor

Although no team member is more important than another, the decision counselor does work most intimately with the decision maker. The counselor is the person who actually takes time to guide the decision maker in his or her decision. This is the function for which you are taking this training. With rare exception, men will counsel other men and boys while women will counsel women and girls. It may be appropriate for both a man and a woman to counsel families making a decision. The counseling session is usually brief—normally 5-15 minutes.

The counselor has five main duties:

1. Clarify the decision.
2. Assist in making a decision by using the Bible and the *Personal Commitment Guide.*[1]
3. Help the decision maker complete the Commitment Record.
4. Introduce the decision maker to the advisor.
5. Lead the decision maker to the presenter.

Presenter

The presenter introduces a decision maker to the congregation. During this presentation, most often accomplished at the end of the service, the presenter will announce the decision maker's name and specify the decision that has been made. This position is usually held by the pastor.

The Commitment Counseling Area

The most effective counseling programs use two different areas: a reception area and a counseling room. The reception area in front of the worship center platform should be used to receive and greet persons coming to make decisions. (See diagram on page 9.) Although some churches use this area for counseling, decision counseling is much more effective if moved to a separate counseling area or room.

Keeping the reception area open for others coming forward is just one advantage of a counseling room. Using a counseling room also allows for better privacy and a more relaxed atmosphere for important conversation between the counselor and decision maker. Being able to move to this type of setting also reduces distractions for both the counselor and decision maker.

Chairs will be arranged into groups of two. Counseling materials such as pencils and *Personal Commitment Guides* should be available at each pair of chairs.

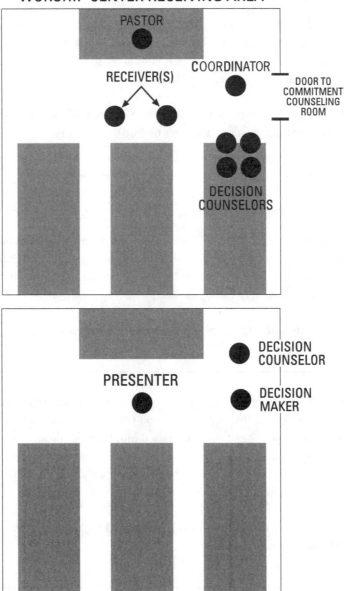

WORSHIP CENTER RECEIVING AREA

Day 2:
What Is the Role of a Decision Counselor?

As you begin today's session, pray for God's guidance as you begin your decision counseling ministry. Ask God to help you learn and apply the principal actions involved in decision counseling. Ask Him for wisdom and understanding as you study and interact with *DecisionTime*.

Let's take a couple of minutes to affirm your own relationship with Jesus. **How do you know that you're a member of God's kingdom?**

_____

_____

Read Matthew 28:19-20: " 'Therefore go and make disciples of all nations, baptizing them in the name of the Father and of the Son and of the Holy Spirit, and teaching them to obey everything I have commanded you. And surely I am with you always, to the very end of the age.' "

How can this passage apply to a decision counselor? _____

_____

According to Matthew 10:32, Jesus calls us to acknowledge Him before men. Paul tells us in Romans 10:9, "That if you confess with your mouth, 'Jesus is Lord,' and believe in your heart that God raised him from the dead, you will be saved."

Every person responding to an invitation has made a decision to accept the inner urging of the Holy Spirit and respond publicly. It is likely that the person will need to make further decisions or clarify the decisions made.

Why do you think that the person will need to make further decisions or clarify the decision made?

_____

_____

As a decision counselor you will need two tools during the counseling time: a Bible and the *Personal Commitment Guide*. The *Personal Commitment Guide* will also be referred to as the *"Guide"* throughout this workbook.

General Guidelines

To be effective, a decision counselor will need to follow a few basic guidelines. If followed, these guidelines will lead to effective counseling. A counselor should prayerfully seek the Lord's hand in anticipation of decisions before the service ever begins. Because you will never become too familiar with the *Personal Commitment Guide,* make a habit of reviewing it prior to every service.

A counselor should always be in the assigned area during the invitation. Keep your eyes open. You need to be aware so you can be where you are needed.

As the counseling session begins you should introduce yourself in a warm and friendly manner. Look nice. Have a breath mint available. You'll want a decision maker's experience to be as pleasant as possible.

Because this is often a time of extreme emotion, take measures to put the decision maker at ease. Use a personal touch—grasp the hand or touch the shoulder. Write the person's name on the Commitment Record as soon as you sit down. That will enable you to address the decision maker by name. Be deliberate in clarifying the decision that the decision maker has been led to make. Time in a counseling session can be fairly brief. A normal session will last about 5-10 minutes, so clarification is very important.

Make sure that the Commitment Record has been completed as the counseling session draws to a close. You will also want to ensure confidentiality of personal information. As a reminder of the commitment that has been made, send home with the decision maker the *Personal Commitment Guide* you have used.

Counseling Session Checklist

Before the Service
- Pray.
- Review the *Personal Commitment Guide*.

During the Invitation
- Be in your assigned place.
- Keep your eyes open. You must know when you are needed.
- You want the total appearance to be pleasant.

As the Counseling Session Begins
- Introduce yourself. Be warm and friendly. Put the decision maker at ease.
- Write the decision maker's name on the Commitment Record in the *Guide*.
- Ask a transition question, "What decision would you like to make?"
- Listen attentively as the decision maker describes the decision.
- Clarify the decision by restating it as you understand it.
- Ask the decision maker to confirm or correct the decision as you have restated it.

During the Counseling Session
- Use your Bible and the *Personal Commitment Guide*.
- Always begin with the Salvation panel.

As the Counseling Session Concludes
- Complete the Commitment Record.
- Tear off the Commitment Record and send the *Guide* with the decision maker as a reminder of his commitment.
- Maintain confidentiality.

After the Counseling Session
- Introduce the decision maker to the advisor.
- Lead the decision maker to the presenter.

Note the action words used in the above guidelines. You may have already noticed that decision counseling is an active process. Look at the general guidelines again and circle every word that describes an action.

When does your participation in decision counseling begin?

Not only does your participation not begin with the counseling session, it doesn't even begin at the same time as the service. Your participation as a decision counselor begins well before the service. Your prayer for the service and those called to make decisions begins your participation for commitment counseling.

Clarifying the Decision
Clarifying the decision is the first priority. The decision maker may not be sure what decision she needs to make. Just after introductions you should use a

transition question for clarification. The first transition question you ask will be a key in determining the decision maker's reason for responding to the invitation.

Listen closely to whatever response is given to your transition question. Below are two transition questions that may help with clarification:

➤ **What decision would you like to make?**

➤ **How may I help you?**

Never assume anything! Listen to the decision maker. Do not interrupt her. Allow her to talk so you can determine the decision that is being made. Being a prayerful listener is very important for effective decision counseling.

Write the transition question you'll be using in the blank below.

_____

Complete this sentence: At the beginning of the counseling session, the counselor

must _____ what decision is being made.

Using the Personal Commitment Guide

Introduce the decision maker to the *Guide*. This is the next step in clarifying the decision. Using different panels, the *Personal Commitment Guide* outlines the counseling process for six different types of decisions. **List the six different decisions listed in the Personal Commitment Guide.**

1. _____

2. _____

3. _____

4. _____

5. _____

6. _____

You will become very familiar with the format of the *Guide* during your study of *DecisionTime*. All the panels are formatted to follow the same, step-by-step outline. **Find the panel of the Guide labeled "Salvation"and complete this review:**

1. Find the two questions printed at the top of the panel.
2. Each panel is divided into these sequenced sections. Complete the title of each section.

God's _____

Our _____

God's _____

Our _____

My _____

Accepting Jesus as Lord and Savior is the most important decision anyone will ever make. As a counselor, you will want to make sure that the decision maker has taken this step. Begin every counseling session with the Salvation panel. Ask the decision maker about his salvation experience. It's important to know that many people join churches, rededicate lives, seek counsel, and even commit to church vocations without having a genuine experience of God's saving grace. The most important decision is placing faith and trust in Christ.

What is the most important decision a person will make in his life? Underline the sentence in the above paragraph which answers this question.

After completing the Salvation panel, review the Baptism, Church Membership, Assurance of Salvation, Rededication to Grow Toward Spiritual Maturity, and Commitment to Vocational Christian Ministry panels on your own.

Day 3:
What Kind of Person Should a
Decision Counselor Be?

In order to begin your decision counseling ministry you must meet certain criteria, or "good counselor" characteristics. Today we will take a look at six personal characteristics needed to be a decision counselor.

A Decision Counselor Must Be a Christian

Before anything else a decision counselor must be a Christian. For obvious reasons, a counselor must be a believer in Christ who has assurance of salvation. He must be a believer in order to understand the supernatural means through which God reveals Himself and His will. A counselor must also be sure of his own salvation; his ultimate destination. **Read 1 John 5:12-13 and write the phrase in this passage that assures believers of their place in heaven.**

_____

Use the space below to describe your assurance of salvation.

_____

_____

A Decision Counselor Must Be a Growing Christian

A decision counselor should be a mentally and emotionally stable Christian who is growing spiritually. Daily Bible study and prayer are essential ingredients for a growing relationship with Christ. A growing Christian is one who is growing in a relationship of love, trust, and obedience with Jesus; one that is part of a dynamic relationship that glorifies God. Spiritual maturity characterizes an effective counselor. If this is not an area in which you are doing well, perhaps now is a good time to make a deeper commitment.

In the previous paragraph, circle the essentials for a growing relationship with Jesus.

Place a check on the line below to indicate the time you spend in Bible study. Place a circle on the line to indicate how much time you spend in prayer.

Rarely   **Now and Then**   **Weekly**   **Daily**

A growing Christian sets aside a daily time in which he seeks the Lord's guidance through prayer and diligent reading of God's Word. If you haven't been a faithful servant in this way now is a great time to begin.

Describe the ways you can see yourself growing spiritually.

If this is an area of your spiritual walk that needs improvement, pause now and ask God in prayer for guidance to spiritual growth.

A Decision Counselor Must Be a Praying Person

Always remember that the Holy Spirit convicts and guides the decision maker. Thus, prayer is a vital part of the life of a counselor. A personal prayer life and prayerful attitude during each counseling experience is a given. There are other specific times when prayer is necessary in addition to your daily prayer and Bible study. You should make a habit of praying before, during, and after a service.

Communication between you and God remains open during a counseling session if your heart is open to Him. The invitation at a worship service is a wonderful time to be in touch with the Holy Spirit.

Which of these specific times should a decision counselor be praying? (Check all that apply.)
- ❏ Before the service
- ❏ During the invitation
- ❏ During the "My Commitment" section of the *Guide*
- ❏ After the decision counseling session

A Decision Counselor Must Possess a Genuine Love of Others

Paraphrase Matthew 22:34-40 in the space below.

_____

_____

In this passage Jesus tells us that loving our neighbors as we love ourselves is second as a way of living only to loving God. **How is it possible to love others the way God loves us—unconditionally?**

_____

_____

This kind of unselfish, pure love can come only through Jesus Christ. The decision counselor must love individuals and be committed to helping them. The most effective decision counseling is done in love. No other quality is more important to counseling than love.

We have been validated by God's love for us through Jesus Christ. He yielded His only Son so that we might have eternal life. Only through the love of Jesus will you be able to love others as He directs—as you love yourself.

Why is it important for a counselor to love others?

_____

_____

A Decision Counselor Must Be a Committed Member of the Church

A counselor should be a member of and actively committed to his own church. As a decision counselor, you should be committed to the importance of the local church in God's plan for His people.

Why is the church so important in God's plan for His people?

_____

_____

Identify the ways you demonstrate commitment to your local church.

_____

_____

A Decision Counselor Must Be Willing to Continue Learning

Yes, a decision counselor needs to be trained and prepared. Even so, there is always room to grow spiritually. Because no two counseling sessions will be the same, as a counselor you must be willing to learn from every session. Helping others make eternal decisions is a responsibility not to be taken lightly. You owe it to the person making the decision to be as prepared and knowledgeable as possible. Taking this course is a good indication of your desire to be prepared.

Read the following description:

John is an active member of his church. He is also a leader of the visitation team and participates in the church's prayer ministry. Since becoming a Christian as a college freshman 10 years ago, John has faithfully prayed and studied his Bible. His desire is to learn to be a growing disciple and a mature church member. He has a very aggressive, task-oriented personality, and he tends to be judgmental of others. John often aggressively confronts fellow church members if they offer an opinion that differs from his.

Referring to the decision counseling prerequisites found on pages 15-18, circle the words in the paragraph that best characterize John's ability to counsel.

List any weak or missing counseling characteristics in John.

_____

Again referring to the list of "good counseling" prerequisites, list those characteristics of John's personality that would be helpful in counseling.

_____

At this time, would you recommend John to be a decision counselor? Why or why not?

_____

You may have noted that John is a Christian who appears to be growing through prayer and daily devotions. That he is active in his church is evidenced by his involvement in prayer ministry and visitation. However, because he is often judgmental and confrontational, you may have concluded that he doesn't possess a great deal of love for others. You also may have observed that he isn't willing to learn or consider ideas that differ from his own.

Now evaluate yourself. Notice under each statement below is a number 1 through 5. Knowing that 5 represents your strongest agreement with the statement, circle the number for each item that you feel accurately reflects your ability as a counselor in this area.

1. I am growing spiritually.

    1   2   3   4   5

2. Prayer is a part of my daily life.

    1   2   3   4   5

3. I am a active church member.

    1   2   3   4   5

4. I love and have concern for others.

    1   2   3   4   5

5. I am open and willing to learn.

    1   2   3   4   5

☆ Draw a star beside the characteristics on which you ranked yourself the highest.

❑ Draw a box around a characteristic in which you have noticed recent improvement.

○ Circle the characteristic you believe to be the weakest in your Christian life.

Feel good about how God has blessed you in these areas. By enrolling in this course you have decided to give Him pleasure by using your God-given attributes to glorify Him. Don't worry if you feel more comfortable about some characteristics than others. You can improve weak areas with prayer, daily Bible reading, and by observing the two greatest commandments set forth by Jesus in Matthew 22:37-40.

DecisionTime Commitment

The effectiveness of this study is dependent on your personal commitment. If you are willing to commit your best efforts toward completing this course and becoming a decision counselor, write a personal commitment and sign it below:

_____

_____

_____

Signature _____ Date _____

If you are not sure if you should serve as a decision counselor, speak with your pastor or *DecisionTime* trainer.

Day 4:
What Are Some Skills a Decision Counselor Uses?

Good listening skills are vital to successful decision counseling. During a counseling session, active listening demonstrates an interest in the person and her decision. Listening skills can be developed and improved. **Read Proverbs 18:13. What does this verse mean to you?**

_____

_____

   The Bible tells us, "He who answers before listening—that is his folly and his shame" (Prov. 18:13). Among other things, this passage suggests that Christians should gain a thorough understanding before drawing any conclusions. Decision counseling is no different.

   In order to lead an effective counseling session you must not only allow the decision maker to describe his decision in full, but listen for clarity as well. Utilizing good listening skills will allow you to "pin down" the decision for clarity. This is good for both the counselor and the decision maker. Attentive listening also displays the love and patience of Christ to a fellow believer.

Barriers to Effective Listening

Regardless of our intentions there are times when listening is difficult. For instance, listening effectively is next to impossible at a loud restaurant during lunch hour. We will sometimes fail to listen because we have drawn conclusions prematurely. Listening is often adversely affected by fatigue, annoying sounds, or drifting thoughts. Here are some barriers to effective listening that can occur during a counseling session:

  • Distraction
  • Excessive talking by the counselor
  • Personal bias towards the decision maker

Identify in the margin some distractions that may adversely affect your ability to listen effectively to a decision maker.

What, if any, personal biases do you have which could hinder effective listening and counseling?

_____

How can you overcome these barriers? Write your own rule for effective listening in the margin.

Better Listening Strategies

Listen with Empathy and Sincerity.
Try to put yourself in the other person's place. A counselor should possess a caring, non-judgmental attitude.

Define empathy. _____

_____

   Empathy is being sensitive to the feelings, thoughts, and experiences of others. Being empathetic will not only show sincerity but will also comfort the decision maker. Feeling empathy will open your heart and allow you to listen with more than just your ears.

Listen with Patience.
Avoid overstating your part of the session. Allow the decision maker time to share personal needs. An occasional period of silence is appropriate. You may also find that the decision maker will take advantage of these short pauses in the session to listen as the Holy Spirit continues to speak. Be patient as God continues to speak to those making decisions for Him. Being a patient listener will allow the decision maker time to consider what God is saying.
Try to remember all of the emotions that were running through your mind when you came forward for a public decision. What were some of your thoughts?

_____

_____

Listen with Your Body.

The language of your body can communicate care and interest. Use the following list of body language tips as a checklist:

✔ Sit up and lean forward. In doing so you're saying, "I'm interested in you."

✔ Make eye contact and maintain it.

✔ Use moderate voice inflections. Avoid a monotone.

Underline the key words found in the body language checklist above.

Body language can also prompt negative reactions. Do not exhibit shock or curiosity with body language or facial gestures. You are there to listen confidentially and facilitate the work of God in the life of the decision maker.

Listen with Objectivity.

Listening objectively requires that you carefully filter any feedback. Feedback is any communication from the decision maker. Feedback can be gathered from questions, comments, or body language. Concentrate on what the decision maker is saying at every level. A good listener realizes that listening is active, two-way communication.

Pay attention to the decision maker's body language. Watch for signs of confusion or frustration and allow ample opportunity for responses to your words. Attentively listen to those responses. Avoid drawing premature conclusions based on your own presuppositions. Be calm. Don't overreact to something with which you disagree. Listening objectively means using only the information given by the decision maker in aiding the decision process.

Circle the action words in the above paragraph. Then write these action words in the first column and use the second column to describe the effect this action word has on listening.

_____	_____
_____	_____
_____	_____
_____	_____
_____	_____

_____   _____

_____   _____

_____   _____

_____   _____

_____   _____

_____   _____

_____   _____

_____

Listen with a Positive Attitude.

Remain positive and show interest even if you have been involved in similar sessions. God is giving you an opportunity to be a part of His work, so enjoy it.

Effective Communication

Decision counseling requires communicating face-to-face. Such one-to-one communication is most often hindered in two ways: unclear religious language and information overload.

Words might not have the same meaning for everyone—especially someone who has never been active in church. Remember that decision makers are responding to the language of the Holy Spirit.

Always clarify any word that the decision maker might not understand. This is especially true of terms such as "saved," "redeemed," "repent," "forgiven," "blood," "cross," and "atonement."

Do not overwhelm the decision maker with information. One glance at the _Personal Commitment Guide_ will tell you that it might be easy to overload someone if you add a lot of additional information. Since you will be giving the _Guide_ to the person for follow up, stick to the _Guide_.

In the margin, compose your own list of words unique to a church setting.

Here are some helpful hints for effective communication:

- Speak directly to the person who has come forward. Use the person's name.
- Know what you want to say and focus on the decision. This is not the time to "chat."
- Be positive and confident. You have the Holy Spirit and the authority of God's Word to help you.
- Don't overwhelm the decision maker with information
- Use precise language. Don't take anything for granted.

How can an effective communicator make good use of language?

_____

In effective communication, the counselor needs to:

Speak _____

Know _____

Be _____

Don't _____

Use _____

Ask God to help you be an effective communicator.

Day 5:
What Are the Steps in Decision Counseling?

The saving grace of Jesus Christ is at the heart of every counseling experience. The gospel of Christ is expressed through the work of the Holy Spirit and recounted in the Bible, God's Word to us. An effective decision counselor will rely heavily on Scripture during a counseling session. Decision makers seek truth. The Bible, God's written Word, is the source of that truth.

Read Hebrews 4:12 below and circle the words that describe the Word of God.

"For the word of God is living and active. Sharper than any double-edged sword, it penetrates even to dividing soul and spirit, joints and marrow; it judges the thoughts and attitudes of the heart."

Why should we use Scripture in decision counseling? _____

_____

Compose a mini-testimony about the role God's Word plays in your life.

_____

_____

Using the *Personal Commitment Guide* will help you keep your Scripture focused on the decision maker's need. Because the Bible is the written Word of God, it has God's authority and instruction. The Bible is the source of God's covenant with us. Today you will learn how to use the *Guide* to inject the Word of God into a counseling session.

Using the Format of the Guide

The *Personal Commitment Guide* is a valuable tool for the counselor. There are six panels in the *Guide*: Salvation, Baptism, Church Membership, Assurance of Salvation, Rededication to Grow Toward Spiritual Maturity, and Commitment to Vocational Christian Ministry. Each of the six panels provides Scripture that supports different parts of the counseling session: "God's Purpose," "Our Need," "God's Provision," and "Our Response."

Use the *Personal Commitment Guide* to complete the following chart. You can use any two panels for each group below. Find one Scripture reference for each panel you choose. This will help you become acquainted with the Guide format.

God's Purpose

Panel _____ Scripture _____

Panel _____ Scripture _____

Our Need

Panel _____ Scripture _____

Panel _____ Scripture _____

God's Provision

Panel _____ Scripture _____

Panel _____ Scripture _____

Our Response

Panel _____ Scripture _____

Panel _____ Scripture _____

Relating Scripture Passages to the Decision Maker

Some decision makers may not be familiar with the Bible. The decision counselor must help the decision maker see how a passage addresses a personal need.

Consider this scenario: Mark is a Christian but grew up in another denomination. He has come forward for church membership but does not see the need for baptism.

Find the Baptism panel in the *Guide*. Although this panel cites many, what are two Scriptures you might use to help Mark see the need for baptism?

1. _____

2. _____

Using the Guide to Explain Scripture

Use the *Guide* to explain with greater clarity the meaning of key Scripture. In the above example, you could read aloud Matthew 10:32: " 'Whoever acknowledges me before men, I will also acknowledge him before my Father in heaven.' "

Circle "acknowledge" as you say, Jesus said we are to acknowledge Him before men. What does acknowledge mean to you? After his response say, One of the reasons we get baptized is to profess Jesus as our Lord and Savior. We need to obey Jesus' command.

You can use the *Guide* to relate directly to a specific purpose, need, provision, and response. The *Guide* will also help you as you relate Scripture passages to the decision maker's decision. Using the *Guide* to explain Scripture is yet another way it can inject the Word of God into a counseling session. There is no better tool for meeting the needs of people than the written Word of God.

How can the *Guide* be used to inject the Word of God into a counseling session?

1. _____

2. _____

3. _____

Read 2 Timothy 3:16-17. Why is Scripture an important part of the decision counseling process?

_____

_____

Time in a counseling session can be fairly brief. A normal session will last about 5-15 minutes. Remember that the *Guide* is your tool to accurate and quick Scripture reference. You do not have to memorize the *Guide*. It is totally acceptable to read aloud from the *Guide*.

Having the *Personal Commitment Guide* helps you to keep your Scripture facts accurate and focuses on the decision maker's need. In many cases, it is better to ask the decision maker to read the Scripture. It is not neccesary for you to memorize any of the Scripture references.

The Counseling Outline

OK, the pastor has concluded his message and extended an invitation. As you pray silently during this part of the service you can feel the presence of the Holy Spirit. After the receivers have taken their places in front of the congregation, a young man slips into the aisle and makes his way to a receiver. After greeting him, the receiver directs this young man to you, the counselor. Here are the steps you should take once the decision maker has been assigned to you.

Get Acquainted
- Introduce yourself. It is helpful to wear a name tag.
- Write the decision maker's name on the Commitment Record.

Clarify the Decision
- Ask a transition question such as, "What decision would you like to make?"
- Listen attentively as the decision maker describes the decision.
- Clarify the decision by restating it as you understand it.
- Ask the decision maker to confirm or correct the decision as you have restated it.

Use the *Personal Commitment Guide*
- Introduce the *Personal Commitment Guide* to the decision maker.
- Begin with the Salvation panel.
- Ask the introductory questions printed at the top of the Salvation panel.
- Verify the decision maker's personal relationship with Jesus as Lord and Savior.
- Direct attention to the panel that best describes the decision maker's decision.

There will be questions printed at the top of each decision panel. We will study each decision panel in greater depth later on in the study.

All of the panels are written in outline format. Noting the outline of the panel, survey the Salvation panel in your *Guide*.

Write the outline points in the blanks below:

1. God's _____

2. Our _____

3. God's _____

4. Our _____

5. My _____

Which two parts of the outline refer to God's part of the decision?

_____

_____

Which three parts of the outline refer to the decision maker's part of the session?

_____

_____

_____

---

[1] To order: WRITE LifeWay Church Resources Customer Service; One LifeWay Plaza; Nashville, TN 37234-0113; FAX order to (615) 251-5933; PHONE (800) 458-2772; EMAIL to *customerservice@lifeway.com;* ORDER ONLINE at *www.lifeway.com;* or VISIT the LifeWay Christian Store serving you.

Week 2

Counseling for Salvation

This week you will learn how to explain to a decision maker the need for salvation and the way to receive Jesus.

Day 1:
God's Purpose

Before you begin Week 2, pray that God will use you to bring lost persons to receive Jesus as Lord and Savior. In Ephesians 1:4 Paul wrote, "For he chose us in him before the creation of the world to be holy and blameless in his sight." Return to this verse throughout the week as you prayerfully learn how to counsel a decision maker for salvation.

You have already learned the introductory steps to counseling for salvation. These steps were presented in the outline found on page 12.

Using the blanks, put these six introductory counseling activities in the correct sequence.

____ Introduce yourself.

____ Ask the decision maker to confirm or correct the decision as you have restated it.

____ Ask a transition question, "What decision would you like to make?"

____ Write the decision maker's name on the Commitment Record.

____ Clarify the decision by restating it as you understand it.

____ Listen attentively as the decision maker describes the decision.

(Check your answers: 1, 6, 3, 2, 5, 4)

Once you've completed these introductory steps and clarified the decision, it's time to begin counseling for salvation.

As you counsel, use your Bible to read the Scripture referenced but not quoted in the *Guide*. Introduce the decision maker to the *Personal Commitment Guide* and turn to the Salvation panel. Underline or circle key words in the *Guide* as you explain them.

Begin every counseling session by asking the two questions found at the top of the Salvation panel. If the person has stated he is coming for salvation, you will use the whole Salvation panel. However, if he comes for another decision, use the Salvation panel as much as is needed to ensure that the decision maker has accepted Christ as his Lord and Savior.

Give your own answers to these questions in the space below.

_____

_____

_____

Questions
➤ Have you come to a place in your life that you know for certain you have eternal life and will go to heaven when you die?
➤ Suppose you were standing before God right now and He asked you, "Why should I let you into my heaven?" What would you say?

Using the Questions

"Have you come to a place in your life that you know for certain you will have eternal life and will go to heaven when you die?"

A person will usually answer the first question by saying either "Yes," "No," or "I'm not sure."

"Yes" generally means that a person is a Christian and sure of salvation. But it is possible that a person may only think he is a Christian. His trust could be in self, good deeds, or church membership. This is why the second question is important.

"No" or "I'm not sure" might suggest one of two conclusions: either the decision maker is not a Christian or he lacks assurance of his salvation. Regardless of what you may believe to be the case, move on to the next question. Question 2 will clarify the person's understanding of salvation.

What would you say if you were standing before God right now and He asked you, "Why should I let you into My heaven?"

People will usually respond to this question in two ways. Either (1) they trust in such things as being a good person, "morality," church membership, baptism, or family heritage, or they (2) trust in what Jesus Christ has done for them through His death and resurrection. The only correct answer is trust in Jesus.

Read this possible scenario and answer the question below: Maria is coming to join the church by transfer of her membership from another church. She answers

Question 1 by saying, "Yes." She responds to Question 2 by saying she "grew up in the church."
As a counselor, how would you proceed?

_____

_____

Your first obligation is to ensure that the decision maker has accepted Christ as her Lord and Savior. Since Maria's salvation is questionable, you should continue using the Salvation panel.

Read the segment of the Salvation panel found under "God's Purpose." Circle the key words in John 3:16 that might be misunderstood.

You should have circled at least the following words in the Guide. These words may be unfamiliar to the decision maker. Use the following definitions to explain them. **List some synonyms in the blanks provided under each word.**

> **God's Purpose**
>
> God loves us and has a purpose for our lives. The Bible states it this way: "For God so loved the world that he gave his one and only Son, that whoever believes in him shall not perish but have eternal life" (John 3:16). God's purpose is that we have eternal life.
> ➤ God gives eternal life as a gift (Rom. 6:23).
> ➤ We can live a full and meaningful life right now (John 10:10).
> ➤ We will spend eternity with Jesus in heaven (John 14:3).

• The World – All people

_____

• Perish – Die and be eternally separated from God

_____

• Eternal – Life that lasts forever

_____

Ask the decision maker: According to John 3:16, what is God's purpose for our lives? Then ask: Why does God want us to have eternal life? **Take a moment to answer these questions for yourself.**

_____

_____

God's purpose for our lives is summarized by the three statements given in the "God's Purpose" section of the *Guide*. You will want to read these truths to the decision maker directly from the *Guide*. As you read, underline the key words in the three statements. For now, underline the key words in the list on page 33.

• God gives eternal life as a gift. Ask the decision maker to read Romans 6:23: "For the wages of sin is death, but the gift of God is eternal life through Christ Jesus our Lord." Ask the decision maker to think about the word *gift*. A person is saved once he has asked Jesus to come into his heart and publicly professed his faith. **Complete this sentence:**

Salvation or eternal life is received _____

Salvation is received by asking Jesus to come into your heart and by accepting His eternal gift.

• We can live a full and meaningful life right now. Jesus said, " 'The thief comes only to steal and kill and destroy; I have come that they may have life, and have it to the full' " (John 10:10). In this verse, Jesus tells us that we can have a full and meaningful life right now. It will be important to emphasize to a decision maker the "here and now" cited in this passage. The gift of Jesus is both timeless and enduring.

• We will spend eternity with Jesus in heaven. " 'And if I go and prepare a place for you, I will come back and take you to be with me that you also may be where I am' " (John 14:3). Jesus is saving a place for everyone who has accepted Him. What an amazing thought! The Savior and Son of God has been saving a place for you and me. Decision makers will need to know that there is an eternity waiting for them. They are not only a part of God's plan on earth, but also a part of a much grander design—an eternal one. Salvation is the "first step" toward God's purpose.

For Practice

As the counseling session begins, Dan says, "I don't see any meaning to life. If God has a purpose for my life, what is it?"

Refer back to the section explaining God's purpose given on page 34.
What would you say to Dan?

_____

_____

_____

    Tomorrow we will concentrate on "Our Need." Before you close today's
session, think for a moment about God's incredible plan.

Day 2:
Our Need

Read the paragraph found on the Salvation panel under "Our Need." This segment of the panel helps the decision maker see how sin separates him from God and prevents him from fulfilling God's purpose.

Underline the first sentence of the "Our Need" section of the *Guide*. This phrase describes the need for salvation. Circle the three bulleted phrases that follow. These key phrases allude to truths found in the Bible concerning our need for salvation.

Our need for salvation is brought about by one thing: sin. We are sinners by nature and by choice. How did we get that way? The answer lies in the story of original sin. For that we can refer to creation itself.

Complete this brief Bible study on the nature of sin. Read each Scripture passage and then circle the correct response.

Our Need

As we search for meaning in life, we discover that our sinful nature keeps us from fulfilling God's purpose for our lives.

➤ We are all sinners by nature and by choice. "For all have sinned and fall short of the glory of God" (Rom. 3:23).

➤ We cannot save ourselves. "For it is by grace you have been saved, through faith—and this not from yourselves, it is the gift of God—not by works, so that no one can boast" (Eph. 2:8-9).

➤ We deserve death and hell. "For the wages of sin is death, but the gift of God is eternal life in Christ Jesus our Lord" (Rom. 6:23).

---

1. Read Genesis 1:26-28; 2:15-17. Adam and Eve . . .

    a. were created with a sinful nature.

    b. were created complete and free to choose to obey or disobey God.

2. Read Genesis 3:1-13. Adam and Eve . . .

    a. were not responsible for their disobedience.

    b. willfully disobeyed God.

3. Read Genesis 3:16-19; Romans 5:12-21; and 1 Corinthians 15:22. The disobedience and resulting fall of Adam and Eve . . .

    a. affected the physical creation.

    b. affected the entire human family.

    c. affected God.

    d. all of the above.

(Answers: 1-b, 2-b, 3-d)

Adam and Eve were created whole, complete, and free to obey or disobey God. They willfully disobeyed God. Their disobedience and fall affected themselves, the world, humanity, and God Himself.

Adam and Eve chose to give Satan a place in their lives. The decision was theirs. The entire human race has been affected by the fall of our first parents, but each person continues to have the choice to obey or disobey God. Each person is responsible for his choices.

Read the following Scripture verses and write in your own words the truths given about our need for salvation:

Romans 3:23

_____

Ephesians 2:8-9

_____

Romans 6:23

_____

How can these verses encourage you?

_____

_____

As you begin the counseling session, ask the decision counselor to read aloud the initial statement given under "Our Need." Ask the decision maker, Why do we need salvation? Circle *sinful nature* in this statement. We need salvation for three reasons:

- We are all sinners by nature and by choice (Rom. 3:23).
- We cannot save ourselves (Eph. 2:9).
- We deserve death and hell (Rom. 6:23).

"Sin," "sinful nature," and "death" may need to be explained. Explaining these terms will help clarify the need for salvation:

- Sin—Thoughts, words, and actions not Christlike in intent or deed; to depart from what is right; missing the mark
- Sinful nature—Our inclination toward sin
- Death—Separation from God; living away from God forever

Circle these words in the *Guide* during a counseling session.

Day 3:
God's Provision

God loves us and has a purpose for our lives. Yet we know that we have sinned and turned away from God. Because of His great love, God has made provision for forgiveness and eternal life.

The Bible makes it clear that all have sinned, that the price of sin is death, and that God can make no exceptions as a holy and righteous God. Instead of exceptions, God has provided atonement for our sins through Jesus Christ. Both God's purpose and God's provision converge in Jesus. He is living proof of God's purpose and provision.

Read Romans 6:23. Identify the two truths found in this verse.

1. _____

2. _____

Because of our sin, we deserve to die and be eternally separated from God. This is the fate that we have earned. However, God has provided for us a gift: eternal life. We do not deserve this gift and we cannot work to earn it. Only out of His love and mercy can we obtain the gift of eternal life.

Read John 1:1-3. What is the relationship of Jesus Christ to God?

_____

What is the relationship between Jesus Christ and creation?

_____

Read John 1:4. What is the relationship between Jesus Christ and life?

_____

Jesus is not less than God or inferior to God—He is God. This is very clear throughout the New Testament. He has always been and always will be. Jesus Christ is the great God Almighty, the Creator of the heavens and earth. Jesus is the source of life.

Read John 1:14. What is the relationship between Jesus Christ and humanity?

_____

God became a man! Although it's difficult for us to comprehend, the great God of the universe became a human being so that He could save us. This is called the incarnation.

Read Romans 4:25. What is the great purpose of Christ coming to earth as a man?

_____

Three truths about God's provision for our salvation are:
1. Jesus is God and became man.
2. Jesus died for us on the cross.
3. Jesus was resurrected from the dead and is alive today.

Jesus came to die. His death on the cross was for a purpose. His death provides evidence of God's love for us as it covers our sins.
   Read the following Scripture passages. Beside each reference write a phrase which explains what the passage teaches about the purpose of Jesus' death.

Isaiah 53:4-6 _____

Romans 5:8 _____

2 Corinthians 5:21 _____

Jesus accepted our pain and suffering. Isaiah tells us that He was "pierced for our transgressions" (Isa. 53:5). In short, He accepted our sin. We were still sinners when He died for us (Rom. 5:8). In fact, "God made him who had no sin to be sin" for our sakes (2 Cor. 5:21). We could be saved only by the perfection of Christ.
   God's provision for our salvation extends beyond the death of Jesus, however. Jesus is alive today. He died on the cross, but He also arose from the grave! Jesus conquered death to complete our salvation. His resurrection justifies us despite our sinful nature. The death and resurrection of Christ means that we do not have to pay the penalty of death for our sin. His atonement reconciles us to God.

What would be your explanation if a decision maker asked you, "Why did Jesus have to die on the cross?"

_____

_____

As you explain God's provision for our salvation to a decision maker, you may need to clarify some terms. **Match each of the following terms with its correct definition.**

__ 1. Word

a. The act of God declaring a person pardoned and forgiven; a right standing or relationship before God.

__ 2. Incarnation

b. The coming to life again of Jesus; His rising from the dead.

__ 3. Atonement

c. Another name for Jesus.

__ 4. Justification

d. God in human form as Jesus.

__ 5. Resurrection

e. The reconciliation between persons and God brought about by the death of Jesus Christ.

(Answers: 1-c, 2-d, 3-e, 4-a, 5-b)

God's Provision

God is holy and just and must punish sin. Yet He loves us and provides forgiveness for our sin. Jesus said, "I am the way and the truth and the life. No one comes to the Father except through me" (John 14:6).

➤ Jesus is God and became man (John 1:1, 14).
➤ Jesus died for us on the cross (1 Pet. 3:18).
➤ Jesus was resurrected (arose) from the dead and is alive today (Rom. 4:25 and 6:9-10).
➤ God, through His Holy Spirit, calls us to Himself (John 6:44).

Use this counseling sequence for the "God's Provision" segment of the Salvation panel.

- Read the initial statement aloud, including John 14:6.
- Read John 1:1 and 1:14. Say, Jesus is God and became a man.
- Read 1 Peter 3:18 and Romans 4:25; 6:8-9 with the decision maker. Ask, What did Jesus do so we could have salvation?
- Ask, Do you understand what Jesus' death and resurrection mean to you as a sinner?

Be sure the decision maker knows that eternal life is a gift from God. A person must accept Jesus to receive this gift. Once the decision maker understands how God provides salvation, he can respond to God's gift. Tomorrow you'll learn how to utilize the "Our Response" part of the *Personal Commitment Guide*.

Day 4:
Our Response

No matter how clearly the other points in the counseling outline have been presented or how well the decision maker has understood, the decision maker remains a non-Christian unless he commits his life to Christ. Salvation does not occur unless the person responds by receiving Jesus as Lord and Savior.

Before we focus on how to help the decision maker receive Christ, let's review the steps in the Salvation panel that you have already learned.

- You have asked the two questions and have clarified the decision.
- You have begun the session with the Salvation panel of the *Guide*.
- You have led the decision maker through the "God's Purpose," "Our Need," and "God's Provision" sections of the Salvation panel.

Read again the paragraph at the top of the page. What determines a person's eternal relationship with God?

_____

As much as God loves us and wants us to have a restored relationship with Him, He will not force Himself on us. Just as we are personally responsible for sin in our lives, we are also personally responsible for choosing to have a right relationship with God. Our eternal relationship with God is determined by our choice to accept Christ.

The Bible teaches us about responding to Jesus. **Read the following Scripture verses and complete the sentences that follow:**

John 1:11-12: In order to become a child of God one must _____

_____

John 3:15: In order to have eternal life a person must _____

_____

Romans 10:13: In order to be saved a person must _____

_____

These three phrases describe the same action—making a commitment to Christ. In order to become a child of God one must willingly receive Him and believe in His name. Eternal life is yours once you become a believer in Jesus Christ. Romans 10:13 reads, "Everyone who calls on the name of the Lord will be saved." All three of these passages have one thing in common: only through Jesus can we be saved.

Conversion is simply "the experience of becoming a Christian." The New Testament describes conversion as turning away from sin and turning to Jesus for salvation. Both the Old and New Testaments refer to conversion experiences. Read Acts 9:35 and 1 Thessalonians 1:9 for examples of New Testament conversion. Jonah 3:10 is an example of an Old Testament conversion experience. **What action describes the conversion in each of these verses?**

In each case, the newly converted have "turned from" a former way of living. A person must turn from his old self in order to have a legitimate conversion experience.

Steps to Receiving Christ

In the "Our Response" section of the Salvation panel, the *Guide* provides three steps for receiving Christ. **Underline these three steps.**

To live in Christ a person must first accept Him. Receiving Christ requires three separate acts. A person must first repent of sin. After repenting, the person needs to place his faith in Jesus. Once a person has put his faith in Jesus he can surrender to Christ as his Lord and Savior.

Your objective in using the "Our Response" section is to help the decision maker understand that salvation is dependent on accepting Jesus. Follow these steps:

Read the opening paragraph including John 1:12. Circle *received* and *believed*.

Our Response

The only way Jesus can affect our lives is for us to receive Him. The Bible says, "Yet to all who received him, to those who believed in his name, he gave the right to become children of God" (John 1:12).
➤ We must repent of our sin. "Repent, then, and turn to God, so that your sins may be wiped out, . . ." (Acts 3:19)
• Repentance is not just feeling sorry for our sin (Acts 26:20).
• Repentance is turning away from our sin and turning to God through Jesus.
➤ We must place our faith in Jesus. "For it is by grace you have been saved, through faith—and this not from yourselves, it is the gift of God" (Eph. 2:8).
• Faith is not just believing facts about Jesus (Jas. 2:19)
• Faith is trusting in Jesus (Rom. 10:11).
➤ We must surrender to Jesus as Lord. "That if you confess with your mouth, 'Jesus is Lord,' and believe in your heart that God raised him from the dead, you will be saved. For it is with your heart that you believe and are justified, and it is with your mouth that you confess and are saved" (Rom. 10:9-10).
• Surrendering to Jesus as Lord is not just saying we give our lives to Jesus (Matt. 7:21)
• Surrendering to Jesus as Lord is giving Jesus control of our lives.

Step One—Repent of Sin

A person regrets sin because of its consequences and feels sorrow because he has sinned against God.

Repentance suggests a profound sorrow for sinning against God, not feeling sorry for your sins.

Read Acts 3:19. According to this verse, repentance is turning to God so your sins may be wiped out. **Use the Guide to fill in the following blanks:**

Repentance is turning away from _____ and turning to God through

_____

When you read Acts 3:19 to the decision maker, circle *repent*. Then, read the statements related to repentance and say, When we repent, we turn away from our sins and turn to Jesus Christ.

Step Two—Place Faith in Christ

The verb form of *faith* is often translated *believe*. In English, *believe* may suggest only the acceptance of fact. For instance, you may "believe" that a person is a good physician, but unless you trust your life to him he cannot help you with his medication or surgery. Both words (*faith* and *believe*) carry the idea of confidence, trust, and dependence. Faith is more than believing a fact. Faith is trusting your life to Jesus (Rom. 10:11). Ephesians 2:8 reads, "For it is by grace you have been saved, through faith—and this not from yourselves, it is the gift of God." To place one's faith in Jesus, a person commits and trusts his life to Him.

How would you define faith? _____

_____

Ephesians 2:8 reminds us that faith is a gift of God. When a person has faith in Christ he has an intimate, God-given relationship with Him. Faith is not a matter of knowledge. If faith were a matter of knowledge, even the demons would place their faith in Jesus (James 2:19).

As you read Ephesians 2:8 to the decision maker, circle *faith* and *gift from God*. Read the two statements about faith in the *Guide* to the decision maker.

Step Three—Surrender to Jesus as Lord

A Christian surrenders his whole life to Jesus. Christ must become Lord of a person's life. **Read Romans 10:9-10 and Matthew 7:21 and explain what it means to say, "Jesus is Lord of my life."**

_____

_____

Lordship means "having power and authority." The lordship of Christ is accomplished by allowing Him to have complete control of our lives. This is done as His Spirit lives in us. Christ is in control through His Spirit.

Help the decision maker understand what is meant by surrender by reading Romans 10:9-10 and underlining *Jesus* and *Lord*. Explain *confess* and *Lord*. *Confess* means "to acknowledge." *Lord* is "ruler," or "master." Read the two bulleted sentences that follow in the *Guide*.

You could use an illustration like the one below to explain *surrender*.

Giving Jesus control is like driving a car. Imagine yourself driving down the highway with another person. As long as you are driving, you are in control. If at some point you say to the other person, "You take the wheel and drive," then the other person will be in control of the driving. In the same way, we turn over the "driving" of our lives to Jesus by saying, "Jesus, You take control of my life, and I will go where You want me to go." In turning over the controls of our lives to Him, we surrender to Jesus as Lord.

The decision maker will now have all the information he needs to make a commitment or decision.

Is Jesus Lord of your life? Take a moment to stop and acknowledge the lordship of Christ in your life. If you need to surrender the "control" to Him, do so now.

For Review

Match each term with its correct definition.

___ 1. Conversion a. to turn from our sin and turn to Jesus
___ 2. Repent b. the experience of becoming a Christian
___ 3. Faith c. to give control
___ 4. Confess d. trust and commitment
___ 5. Lord e. ruler; master
___ 6. Lordship f. to state or give testimony to; to acknowledge
___ 7. Surrender g. authority or power

(Answers: 1-b, 2-a, 3-d, 4-f, 5-e, 6-g, 7-c)

Day 5:
My Commitment

Understanding how to receive Christ is not enough. Each decision maker must choose to make a commitment. As a counselor, you already know that a person's commitment to Christ is the most important decision he will ever make. Not coincidentally, this portion of the session is the most significant part.

Read Romans 10:13. What does "call upon the name of the Lord" mean?

Read Revelation 3:20. Who "opens the door"? Explain to the decision maker that we can call on the Lord through prayer. Praying is talking to God. Use the first paragraph of the "My Commitment" segment as a transition. Answer any questions.

Then, ask these three questions:
- "Does what we have been discussing make sense to you?"
- "Is there any reason why you would not be willing to receive God's gift of eternal life?"
- "Are you willing to turn from your sin, place your faith in Jesus right now, and give Him control of your life right now?"

My Commitment

Giving Jesus control is something each person must do for himself or herself. No one else can make this decision for you. Jesus says, " 'Here I am! I stand at the door and knock. If anyone hears my voice and opens the door, I will come in and eat with him, and he with me' " (Rev. 3:20).
➤ Does what we have been discussing make sense to you?
➤ Is there any reason you would not be willing to receive God's gift of eternal life?
➤ Are you willing to turn from your sin, place your faith in Jesus, and give Him control of your life right now?
If you are willing to receive Jesus into your life now, you can invite Him in by prayer. You may use the following prayer or a similar one using your own words:
"Dear Lord Jesus, I believe You are the Son of God and died to forgive me of my sins. I know I have sinned. I ask You to forgive me. I turn from my sins, and I receive You as my Lord and Savior. Thank You for saving me. I want to live for You the rest of my life. Amen."

The decision maker can answer the first question in two ways: "Yes" or "No." If he responds with "Yes," ask the next question. If he answers "No," however, you should first identify the place at which the misunderstanding occurs and return to that section of the *Guide*.

A decision maker may respond to the second question in a number of ways. Many will answer, "No, there is no reason for being unwilling to receive God's free gift." But there will be some decision makers who will cling to the notion that there are certain circumstances that prevent a person from receiving this gift. These circumstances will vary from person to person and are virtually infinite.

If this is the case, return to the "Our Response" section. Read again John 1:12 and Acts 3:19. Depend on God's Word and the Holy Spirit to convince and convict.

If the decision maker is willing to turn from his sin and place his faith in Jesus right now, move on to the prayer of commitment.

There will always be some that will want to wait before answering the third question affirmatively. You can expect some decision makers to respond by offering answers such as "I'm still not ready," "I'm not sure," or "I don't understand." Be patient. Allow the person to respond to the leading of the Holy Spirit. If the decision maker does not seem to be ready to make a decision, do not push him or her to "pray the prayer." State that someone will be following up later.

Share the *Guide's* example of a prayer of commitment with the decision maker. Invite the decision maker to pray this prayer by repeating after you as you pray the prayer, phrase by phrase. After the prayer of commitment affirm the person for his commitment.

Then, continue with the Baptism and Church Membership panels.

Counseling for Salvation: Final Actions

When you are ready to end the counseling session, complete these actions:

1. Complete and detach the Commitment Record. Explain to the decision maker that this card allows the church to provide follow-up ministry.

2. Give the rest of the *Personal Commitment Guide* to the decision maker as a reminder and review of the decision. Encourage the decision maker to keep this *Guide* in her Bible.

3. Take the decision maker back to the advisor and introduce her.

4. Pray for this new Christian each day during the following week.

Review the five-point counseling outline used in the Guide and then fill in the blanks below.

1. God's _____

2. Our _____

3. God's _____

4. Our _____

5. My _____

Remember that the decision maker will want affirmation of his decision. As a counselor, part of your job will be assuring him of his part in God's plan. God loves us and has a plan for our lives. His purpose is that we have eternal life as a free gift. We can live a full and meaningful life right now in Christ. Once saved, we can be assured of all these things—plus an eternity with the Father in heaven.

God's provision is through Jesus Christ. Because the wages of our sin is death, we deserve to die. But God has given us a chance to choose eternal life. God's provision of eternal life is available only one way: Jesus Christ.

What are the steps to receiving Christ? Use the "Our Response" section of your Guide if you have trouble remembering. Remember, you will have the Guide handy during a session as well.

1. _____

2. _____

3. _____

Practice: Ask a friend or family member to role play an unsaved person to help you as you practice your commitment counseling skills.

Remember to:
- Begin with the introductions.
- Discern the decision being made by asking the opening questions.
- Lead the decision maker through the "God's Purpose," "Our Need," "God's Provision," "Our Response," and "My Commitment" sections of the *Personal Commitment Guide*. Use your Bible as needed.

WEEK 3

Baptism and Church Membership

This week you will learn the biblical basis for both baptism and church membership. If the decision maker has come forward for salvation, use the entire Salvation panel. However, if a person comes to make another decision, use the Salvation panel until you are sure he has received Jesus as Lord and Savior.

Day 1:
The Biblical Basis of Baptism

Read Matthew 28:19. Jesus has charged all Christians to make disciples and baptize all nations. Before you become involved with Week 3, thank God for the benefits of belonging to the body. Pray that God will lead believers to follow Him in baptism.

   The significance of baptism in the church can be summarized in these four statements:
   1. Baptism symbolizes the death, burial, and resurrection of Christ.
   2. Baptism symbolizes the believer's death to the consequences of sin, the death of his old life, and his new life with Christ.
   3. Baptism is an act of obedience and commitment to Christ.
   4. Baptism identifies the believer publicly with Christ and the local fellowship of believers. It is a prerequisite for church membership.

In each of the above statements, underline the key phrase that describes a function of baptism.

   Find each of the following Scriptures in your Bible: Romans 6:3-5, Matthew 28:19-20, Acts 2:41, and Acts 9:18. **Match each of the above summary statements** with the Scripture that supports it. (Some of the statements may be supported by more than one Scripture reference and some of the references may teach more than one truth.)

___ Statement 1   a. Romans 6:3-5
___ Statement 2   b. Matthew 28:19-20
___ Statement 3   c. Acts 2:41
___ Statement 4   d. Acts 9:18
___ Statement 5

Possible answers: 1-a; 2-a; 3-b,c,d; 4-c; 5-a.

Baptists believe that immersion is the only appropriate means of baptism. Here are three facts that give a biblical basis for immersion:
1. Baptism comes from the Greek word that means "to immerse; to dip; to submerge."
2. New Testament accounts of baptisms show that immersion was the practice of both John the Baptist and the early church (Mark 1:9-10, Acts 8:38-39).
3. According to Romans 6:3-5, baptism by immersion symbolizes the believer's identification with the death, burial, and resurrection of Christ.

As a believer, explain why you were baptized. _____

_____

Have you been baptized by immersion since receiving Jesus as Lord and Savior?

Baptism is a response of obedience to Jesus Christ as Lord (Acts 2:38, 41). Although baptism does not save, it demonstrates our recognition of the lordship of Jesus over every aspect of our lives. "Therefore go and make disciples of all nations, baptizing them in the name of the Father and of the Son and of the Holy Spirit, and teaching them to obey everything I have commanded you. And surely I am with you always, to the very end of the age"(Matt. 28:19-20).

A person can be saved only through Jesus Christ. Baptism reflects the symbolic resurrection of a believer and also serves as a public profession of faith. Use the Baptism panel of the *Guide* when you are counseling a person for baptism.

The first section of the Baptism panel is shown here. The question found at the top of this panel should express the importance of baptism to the believer.

Read the first paragraph of the Baptism panel. Circle these three key phrases: "response of obedience," "does not save," and "demonstrates our recognition of the lordship of Christ."

Read the first statement given under "God's Purpose" aloud to the decision maker. Then read Acts 2:41; 8:35-38; and 16:25-34. These three passages from Acts will explain the testimonial aspect of baptism.

Read the next statement and the accompanying scriptural reference (Rom. 6:3-5). This part of the session will provide illustrations for baptism.

Use the "God's Purpose" section to help the decision maker see that baptism . . .

- Is a testimony of a person's salvation experience.
- Is a visual demonstration of what Jesus did to provide us with salvation.

Be sure to emphasize that baptism is symbolic and provides no salvation in itself.

God's Purpose

➤ We declare our new life in Christ through baptism (Acts 2:41; 8:35-38; 16:25-34).

➤ The death, burial, and resurrection of Jesus, as well as our own spiritual death, burial, and resurrection, are portrayed in baptism (Rom. 6:3-5).

Day 2:
Baptism

The Bible makes it clear that every believer should be baptized. Baptist churches require the following persons to be baptized before becoming church members:
- New believers.
- Persons who have accepted Christ as their Lord and Savior but were baptized earlier than that.
- Persons who have been saved but never baptized by immersion.

Some Baptist churches do not accept believers from other denominations by statement. As a counselor, you'll need to know who is able to join your church only by baptism and who may join by statement of their baptism as a testimony of their faith. Ask your pastor or other staff member for clarity on this issue.

Our church's baptism policy: _____

_____

_____

Our Need
➤ We need to confess Jesus publicly through baptism soon after we are saved (Matt. 10:32).
➤ We need to obey Jesus' command (Matt. 28:19).
➤ We need to follow Jesus' example (Matt. 3:13-15).
➤ We need to join the fellowship of the church family (Acts 2:41).

Read the "Our Need" section of the *Personal Commitment Guide* provided below and circle the action word in each statement.

You should have circled "confess," "obey," "follow," and "join." These key words represent the heart of our need to be baptized.

Read the four statements given under "Our Need" to the decision maker. Ask him to circle the four action verbs in the statements and then move on to the "God's Provision" section of the *Guide*. If you notice hesitation on the part of the decision maker, or sense that he might have a question, you can use the Scripture passages given after each statement.

Ask the decision maker to read the first statement from the "God's Provision" section of the *Guide*. Read Mark 1:9-11. Say, Jesus has set the example for us.

Read the second statement and ask the decision maker to circle the term that describes the biblically prescribed method of baptism. Read Mark 1:10.

Read the third statement aloud. Ask the decision maker, Who has given authority to the church to baptize? Read Matthew 28:19-20.

Ask the decision maker to read the first statement from the "Our Response" section of the *Guide*. Explain that an individual must request baptism.

Ask the decision maker to underline phrases in the next two statements which explain what his baptism will do (express her obedience to Jesus and provide a witness/influence to others of her new faith).

In your next group session, your trainer will clarify your church's policy concerning baptism.

God's Provision
➤ Jesus began His public ministry with baptism (Mark 1:9-11).
➤ Jesus demonstrated that immersion in water (being placed under water) is the proper way to be baptized (Mark 1:10).
➤ Jesus has given authority to His followers to baptize (Matt. 28:19).

Our Response
➤ Request a local church to baptize you.
➤ Be baptized as an expression of obedience to Jesus (Acts 2:41).
➤ Influence others through your baptism (Acts 16:31-33).

My Commitment

In summary, the essentials of baptism are:
➤ Believe in Jesus for salvation.
➤ Ask a local church for baptism.
➤ Be immersed in water, showing your identification with Jesus and His church.

If you are willing to take this step of public commitment to Jesus, you can express that willingness through the following or a similar prayer:

"Father, I want to obey You and let others know I have a new life in Jesus Christ. Bless me as I follow Jesus in baptism."

Lead the decision maker in the prayer of commitment. This is done best by asking the decision maker to repeat each phrase after you.

At this point you will move on to a review of the church membership panel with the decision maker.

Practice: Suppose that Glenn has received Christ as Lord and Savior and asks this question, "Why does God want me to be baptized?" **How would you respond to Glenn's question?**

Day 3:
The Biblical Basis for Church Membership

Two different counseling situations require "counseling for church membership" skills. You will use the Church Membership panel if a person comes forward to join your church. But you will also use the Church Membership panel anytime a person makes a decision to receive Christ.

Read Matthew 16:18 and Ephesians 5:25. From these verses, how would you describe Jesus' commitment to the church?

_____

_____

The New Testament teaches us about both the privilege and the responsibility of being a part of the fellowship of believers. Anyone who accepts His message can be baptized. As a believer, you should devote yourself to biblical teaching, fellowship, prayer, and breaking bread (Acts 2:41-42,47).

The New Testament teaches that Christ founded the church. The term "church" has two meanings. First, the church is a local body of baptized believers who have covenanted together to carry out the mandates of the gospel. Second, the church is the body of Christ that includes the redeemed from all the ages.

Counseling for church membership is usually brief. First, ask the questions found at the top of the Church Membership panel. Tell the decision maker that one of the ways we express our commitment to Jesus is through being an active member of the local church. Ask the decision maker, Who built the church?

_____

Are you an active member of a local church? Where?

Jesus built the church (Matt. 16:18) and gave Himself for the benefit of the church (Eph. 5:25).

The church is made up of God's people. To love Jesus is to love His church.

_____

God's Purpose

We can be a part of God's work through the church. "So in Christ we who are many form one body, and each member belongs to all the others" (Rom. 12:5).

➤ As a part of the church, we can worship with other Christians (Heb. 10:25; Eph. 5:19-20).

➤ As a part of the church, we can evangelize, that is, share our faith (Acts 1:8; 2 Cor. 5:18-20).

➤ As a part of the church, we can grow in discipleship to become the kind of people God wants us to be (2 Pet. 3:18).

➤ As a part of the church, we can minister to one another (1 Cor. 12:12-26).

➤ As a part of the church, we can fellowship with one another (Heb. 10:24-25).

Read the first statement of the "God's Purpose" section. Lead the decision maker in reading Romans 12:5. Circle "one body" in the *Guide*.

Read the other five statements aloud. Circle *worship, evangelize, discipleship, fellowship,* and *minister*. Identify these actions as the five functions of the church. If time permits, read the accompanying Scripture passages. If time does not permit, encourage the decision maker to read them later.

Read the following Scripture passages. Identify the essential church function that each passage describes.

1. Ephesians 5:19-20 _____

2. 2 Corinthians 5:18-20 _____

3. 2 Peter 3:18 _____

4. Hebrews 10:24-25 _____

5. 1 Corinthians 12:12-26_____

Our Need

➤ We need to identify publicly with the family of God (Acts 2:41-42).

➤ We need strength for daily living, which comes through fellowship with other Christians (Heb. 3:13).

➤ We need to express our personal talents and spiritual gifts in service through the church (Rom. 12:4-8).

Refer to the first bulleted statement in the "Our Need" section of the *Guide*. This illustrates the need for fellowship with other Christians in a church setting. Read Acts 2:41-42 to emphasize the importance of joining the church.

Read the remaining two statements in this section. Underline "identify publicly," "strength for daily living," "fellowship with other Christians," and "express our personal talents and spiritual gifts."

Read the first three statements in this

section. These statements will help the decision maker see that God established the church to help believers. God expects believers to be actively involved in the church.

Circle "God established," "God provides," and "God encourages" as you read the first three statements.

Emphasize the last statement by reading Luke 4:16. Underline "Jesus set the example."

We will continue with "Our Response" and "My Commitment" in Days 4 and 5. For now, take time to thank God for establishing His church.

God's Provision

➤ God established the church as the body of Christ (Eph. 4:4; Col. 1:18).
➤ God provides for church membership through the invitation of the local church (Rev. 22:17).
➤ God encourages every Christian to participate in church membership (Heb. 10:25).
➤ Jesus set the example for us through His custom of regular synagogue attendance (Luke 4:16).

Day 4:
Church Membership for the New Christian

Realize that church membership is a relationship closely tied to baptism. Baptist churches require all new believers to be baptized before assuming full church membership. There are three primary ways by which a church receives new members:

- By profession of faith in Christ and baptism by immersion.
- By a statement that claims a person is a Christian and that he has been baptized by a local church of like beliefs and practices.
- By transfer of church membership from one Southern Baptist church to another Southern Baptist church.

Our Response
➤ You may become a member of the local church fellowship by professing your faith and by being baptized (Acts 2:41,47).
➤ You may share the fellowship of the local church by joining its membership.
➤ You may join a church by a statement that you have been baptized by a local church of like beliefs and practices.

Use the initial statement in the "Our Response" section of the Church Membership panel to introduce the requirements for church membership. Go ahead and underline this statement in the paragraph above. Read the second and third statements out loud. Point out that a person who is a member of a Southern Baptist church may transfer membership to another Southern Baptist church.

You'll need to explain your church's policy with clarity if the decision maker is joining the church by statement.

Lead the decision maker in the prayer of commitment. After completing and detaching the Commitment Record, give the rest of the *Guide* to the decision maker as a reference.

Tell the person about ministries such as Sunday School and discipleship experiences. Invite her to be a part of these. Give particular information about your church's new member class.

My Commitment

If you are ready to make the commitment to join the fellowship of the local church, you may do so by expressing your intention on the attached commitment card. Seal your commitment in a prayer similar to the following:

"Dear Lord, thank you for the church, and particularly for this local church. Help me to be a faithful church member and support my church family."

What is your church's plan for follow-up of new Christians and other new church members? (Your group leader can help you complete this.)

_____

_____

_____

Which of your church's ministries will you mention to new members?

_____

_____

_____

_____

_____

Day 5:
Transferring Membership

Many Baptist churches require all believers coming from other denominations to be baptized again. This is done for several reasons. The person may have been baptized as a baby. Some mode or method of baptism other than immersion, such as sprinkling, may have been used. Even when immersion was administered, some meaning may have been attached to it that Baptists do not hold. For example, some denominations believe that baptism is essential to salvation.

Some Baptist churches accept believers from other denominations for membership by statement, some do not, and some address this issue on a case-by-case basis. Your church needs to define clearly for you exactly who qualifies for church membership.

What is your church's policy on accepting new members by statement?

_____

_____

_____

A counselor should be prepared to counsel anyone seeking membership from another denomination. Our goal is to show Christian love and understanding to anyone seeking to be a member of the body of Christ. These guidelines are helpful when counseling someone from another denomination:
- Maintain a Christlike attitude at all times.
- Be respectful and courteous.
- Do not be negative, judgmental, or argumentative.
- Focus on the person and the work of Jesus Christ, not denominational facts.
- Use the Salvation panel of the *Guide* to make a positive presentation of the gospel.

There are three appropriate follow-up actions if the decision maker will be changing denominations:
1. Enroll the person in the new church member class.
2. Present a book on Baptist doctrine to the decision maker (such as *Foundations of the Faith: Basics for Baptists*).
3. Pray for the decision maker.

Caution: If the decision maker is a member of a cult or a religious group that is unfamiliar to you, enlist the pastor's help.

Practice: Imagine that you are counseling a lady who has been a Christian for quite some time, but she belongs to a Southern Baptist church in another state.

What steps would you follow to counsel her decision for church membership?

_____

_____

_____

_____

Did you start with the Salvation panel? We must never assume a person is a believer, even if that person has been a church member for a long time. Did you include a review of the Baptism panel as well as the Church Membership panel?

Week 4

Assurance of Salvation

During Week 4 you will develop skills for counseling a decision maker for assurance of salvation. These skills will prove helpful when counseling a believer with doubts about salvation. At the conclusion of this week you will understand the biblical basis for assurance of salvation.

Day 1:
God's Purpose

"He who has the Son has life; he who does not have the Son of God does not have life. I write these things to you who believe in the name of the Son of God so that you may know that you have eternal life" (1 John 5:12-13). Pray that any who have doubts about salvation will seek and find the assurance God desires for them. Thank God for your own salvation and the assurance that you have.

One of the most vital steps in this counseling ministry is discerning the decision the decision maker needs to make. Begin every counseling session by asking the two questions found at the top of the Salvation panel. If the person has stated he is coming for salvation, you will use the whole Salvation panel. However, if he comes for another decision, use the Salvation panel as much as is needed to ensure that the decision maker has accepted Christ as his Lord and Savior.

If a decision maker indicates a desire for assurance of salvation, do not move immediately to the Assurance of Salvation panel. When a person doubts his or her salvation there is always the possibility that he never accepted Christ as Lord and Savior. As a counselor you will want to discern between the need for assurance of salvation and the need to make a conversion decision.

Use the statements below to help you determine which panel to use if the decision maker has expressed doubt about salvation:
- Tell me about your conversion experience.
- How old were you when you accepted Christ?

• Where did your conversion occur?

• Did you start growing as a Christian after your experience?

If responses to these statements are vague, there is a possibility that the person has never been saved. Use the Salvation panel if this is the case. If you decide the decision maker needs assurance about his or her salvation, lead the decision maker through the Assurance of Salvation panel of the *Personal Commitment Guide* after a brief review of the Salvation panel.

Your goal is to convince the decision maker that God wants all believers to have assurance of salvation. Ask the question given at the top of the Assurance of Salvation panel: "Do you doubt your salvation?"

Read the first statement in the "God's Purpose" section and ask the decision maker to read aloud 1 John 5:12-13. Ask the decision maker to underline the last phrase of this verse. For now, underline this phrase in your *Guide*. **Ask, To whom are these words written?**

_____

_____

Do you doubt your salvation?

God's Purpose

➤ God wants us to know we have eternal life. The Bible says, "He who has the Son has life; he who does not have the Son of God does not have life. I write these things to you who believe in the name of the Son of God so that you may know that you have eternal life" (1 John 5:12-13).

➤ God wants us to experience the joy of salvation (John 15:10-11).

_____

How about you? Do you know you have eternal life?

_____

How do you know?

_____

Read John 15:10-11. Ask, What does God intend for us to experience? Take a moment to think about how you would answer this question. It is important for you as a counselor to be able to empathize with the decision maker. Tomorrow we will take a look at some of the factors that may lead to a lack of assurance.

What does "joy of salvation" mean to you? _____

_____

_____

Day 2:
Our Need

Has there been a time when you had doubts about your relationship with God? Did you need assurance of your salvation? **Describe a time when you may have doubted your relationship with Him.**

_____

_____

_____

Even the godliest of people may at times express doubt about their relationship to God. **Read these Scripture verses and fill in the chart.**

Scripture	Doubting Person(s)	Occasion
Matthew 28:16-17	_____	_____
John 20:24-25	_____	_____

There are several reasons persons sometimes have doubts about their relationship with God.

Inadequate Guidance

Some believers do not receive any follow-up training after making the initial commitment. Inadequate guidance such as little or no follow-up training can leave a new convert vulnerable to doubt. Two options to suggest for follow-up in your church are a new member class and regular discipleship experiences.

Poor Devotional Life

Failure to manage a regular habit of Bible study, prayer, and worship leads to a poor devotional life. The result of a weak devotional life is a lack of spiritual growth. From spiritual immaturity often springs a lack of assurance. (This subject will be addressed in greater depth during Week 5.)

Inconsistent Living

Living in a way that is inconsistent with Jesus' desires can also lead to doubt. Doubts about salvation will almost always arise in a person that is under the bondage of sin. A person who is not consistently sharing her faith may begin to question whether she finds witnessing difficult because she doesn't have a genuine faith to share.

Improper Teaching

Some new Christians receive inadequate or erroneous teachings. Improper teaching may be given by your church as well as by different cults. False teachings of cults can influence a believer and cause uncertainty and confusion. Because the church can neglect to teach otherwise, some new Christians will believe life to be easy and free of conflict or strife once they are saved. These new believers become frustrated and fall out of the church once they discover that conflict and difficulty continue.

Our Need

Doubts are not uncommon to Christians. Satan wants us to doubt and may plant doubts in our minds (Gen. 3:1). Even the biblical writers experienced doubts and expressed the need for renewal (Ps. 51:12). There are five major factors which cause believers to doubt:

➤ You may not have received adequate explanation when you first believed.

➤ You may have neglected prayer, Bible study, and worship.

➤ You may have allowed sin, disobedience, or a failure to share your faith to cloud your relationship with Jesus.

➤ You may have inadequate or erroneous understanding about God or about your daily Christian life.

➤ You may be experiencing physical or emotional difficulties which are causing you to doubt your salvation.

Physical or Emotional Problems

If a counseling session indicates physical or psychological problems present in the decision maker, do what you can to help the person experience assurance of salvation. Then, advise the person to meet with the pastor or other trained counselor. Ask permission to brief the pastor or counselor in such circumstances.

As a counselor, you should be aware that Christians who have a standard of sinless perfection for themselves will very often feel doubt in their relationship with the Father. These Christians may feel they were never truly saved when they inevitably fall short of perfection.

Place an asterisk (*) by any of these five reasons that have caused you to doubt your salvation. Then, write below how God helped you to have assurance.

_____

_____

_____

Begin the "Our Need" section by asking the opening question in this section of the *Guide*. After the decision maker's response, read the statement that follows the opening question and Psalm 51:12 to her. Continue by asking the next questions. Be sure to read Genesis 3:1 at the appropriate time. It's important that the decision maker know that doubt is the work of Satan.

Ask the decision maker to circle any of the causes that could have contributed to her doubt.

Day 3:
God's Provision

God provides assurance of salvation for every believer. **Read the following Scriptures and answer this question for each one: How does this verse provide assurance to you as a believer?**

Philippians 1:6 _____

John 5:24 _____

John 10:28 _____

Romans 8:16 _____

The above verses illustrate God's two key provisions for our assurance: His Word and the testimony of the Holy Spirit. Assurance of salvation is not based on emotions, memorization, church background, or Christian service. Assurance of salvation is accomplished only through God's provision. A Christian doesn't have to look farther than the Bible for assurance of salvation.

Begin "God's Provision" by reading Philippians 1:6 and the statement that introduces the section.

Ask the decision maker what God promises in Philippians 1:6. Next, lead the decision maker through the remaining three statements of the "God's Provision" section. Use the accompanying Scripture references the following way:

- Use John 5:24 to identify the Bible as the source of assurance.
- Use John 10:28 to identify the enduring promise of eternal life.
- Use Romans 8:16 to identify the work of the Holy Spirit in giving assurance.

God's Provision
➤ God has promised to complete His work of salvation in us (Phil. 1:6).
➤ Jesus promises assurance of eternal life: "Whoever hears my word and believes him who sent me has eternal life and will not be condemned; he has crossed over from death to life" (John 5:24).
➤ Jesus said no one could take the Christian out of His hand (John 10:28).
➤ The Holy spirit tells us we are the children of God (Rom. 8:16).

Day 4:
Our Response and My Commitment

Assurance is accepted by faith and expressed through obedience. Accepting God's assurance of salvation is the choice of every believer. There are four actions of faith that lead to accepting God's assurance: confess, commit, claim, and obey.

Read the following passages. Match the correct Scripture reference with the step in receiving God's assurance of salvation it provides.

___ 1. Confess all known sin

___ 2. Commit yourself to the lordship of Jesus Christ

___ 3. Claim God's promise of salvation by faith

___ 4. Obey God's commands

a. Romans 10:9-10

b. John 14:21

c. 2 Timothy 1:12

d. John 15:10

e. 1 John 1:9

(Answers: 1-e; 2-a; 3-c; 4-b,d)

Our Response

We receive God's assurance by faith and express it through obedience (1 John 2:3-5). Christians are not to trust only their feelings. We walk by faith, not by sight (2 Cor. 5:7). Four actions can bring us to assurance:

➤ Confess all known sin. "If we confess our sins, he is faithful and just and will forgive us our sins and purify us from all unrighteousness" (1 John 1:9).

➤ Commit yourself to the lordship of Jesus Christ (Rom. 10:9-10).

➤ Claim God's promise of salvation by faith. Know. Believe. Entrust. (2 Tim. 1:12).

➤ Obey God's commands (John 14:21; 15:10).

My Commitment

Are you ready to take the four faith actions which bring assurance of salvation? If so, you may want to pray the following or a similar prayer now:

"Father, I place my complete faith in you: I confess to you any sin (you may want to name known sins); I commit myself to the lordship of Jesus; I claim your promise of assurance; and I will live in obedience to your commands. Thank you for the assurance of my salvation."

After reading the first statement in the "Our Response" section, find 1 John 2:3-5 and read it aloud. Make it clear that assurance is not based on emotions, church background, or Christian service.

Read 2 Corinthians 5:7. Ask the decision maker to underline "by faith" in the *Guide*.

Stress the need for confession and forgiveness in the life of all Christians. Read 1 John 1:9 and point out God's faithfulness and His readiness to forgive our sin. Ask the decision maker to circle these three terms: "confess," "forgive," and "purify."

Continue this pattern with the other three statements and verses given in "Our Response." Ask the decision maker to draw a box around the four "faith actions" needed for assurance of salvation: confess, commit, claim, and obey. Ask the decision maker if she is ready to accept God's provision for assurance of salvation and make a commitment. If so, lead her in the commitment prayer.

Day 5:
Time to Review

You have now been exposed to the fundamental skills and basic instruction of decision counseling. So far you have taken a close look at the Salvation, Baptism, Church Membership, and Assurance of Salvation panels of the *Personal Commitment Guide*. Before we begin the next panel, let's review what you have learned so far. Complete the following review activities.

What qualities are needed in order to be an effective counselor?
(Week 1, Day 3) A decision counselor must . . .

_____   _____

_____   _____

_____   _____

There are six decision panels in the *Guide*. They are:

_____   _____

_____   _____

_____   _____

Each panel is divided into five sections:

God's _____

Our _____

God's _____

Our _____

My _____

Listening is a vital skill for decision counseling. Identify the good listening strategies discussed in Week 1, Day 4:

- Listen with _____ and _____

- Listen with _____

- Listen with your _____

- Listen to _____

- Listen with a _____   _____

Mark the following statements true or false. (Week 2, Day 2)

__ A. We are all sinners.

__ B. We cannot save ourselves.

__ C. We deserve death and hell.

What are God's provisions for our salvation? If you need help, look back to the "God's Provision" section of the Salvation panel.

A. Jesus is _____ and became _____.

B. Jesus _____ for us on the cross.

C. Jesus was _____ from the dead.

List the three steps a decision maker must take to receive Christ. (See the "Our Need" section of the Salvation panel.)

1. _____

2. _____

3. _____

Why do we baptize by immersion? (See Week 3, Day 1)

_____

_____

Put a check beside the persons listed below who should be baptized before becoming a member of your church. (See Week 3, Day 2)

____ Church members who have never truly received Jesus as their personal Lord and Savior

____ New believers

____ Believers who transfer membership from another Baptist church of like beliefs and practices

____ Persons who have been saved but never baptized

____ Persons coming from denominations which are not of like beliefs and practices

Week 5

Rededication to Grow Toward Spiritual Maturity

At the conclusion of this week you will understand the nature of rededication, the meaning of spiritual transformation, and how to assist decision makers in a counseling session.

Day 1: The Lordship of Christ

Begin every counseling time by asking the two questions found at the top of the Salvation panel. If the decision maker has come forward for salvation, use the entire Salvation panel. However, if a person comes to make another decision, use the Salvation panel until you are sure he has accepted Jesus as Lord and Savior.

Pray that the Holy Spirit will bring conviction to any church members who are out of fellowship with God. Ask God for guidance as you seek a greater commitment to the lordship of Jesus Christ.

Scripture teaches us that God desires a meaningful, intimate, continually deepening relationship with each of His children. As our relationship with God matures, He transforms us more and more into the likeness of Christ.

At times a believer might find himself having a weakened relationship with God. Upon realizing this, there is often a desire to rededicate his life to the lordship of Christ. By "lordship" we mean the authority and power of our Savior—Jesus Christ.

What does "rededicate" mean to you? _____

_____

Used within the context of the church, *dedicate* means "to set apart and consecrate to God and to His purpose." Not coincidentally, *rededication* is the act of dedicating again.

Believers rededicate their lives to Christ for many reasons. A decision for rededication is not always the result of unconfessed sin. Other factors may also lead to
rededication. Some of the more common reasons are:

- Situations relating to work, relocation, births and deaths, or illnesses.
- Special occasions such as a new year, anniversary, or tragedy.
- A desire to grow spiritually.
- A lack of daily devotion time.
- Specific sin.
- A gradual drifting away from Christ. Drifting occurs when lack of concern
  and apathy have taken away the believer's joy, peace, and fulfillment.

**Have you ever rededicated your life to the lordship of Christ—publicly or
privately?   ☐ Yes ☐ No**

If yes, briefly explain the circumstances surrounding your rededication.

_____

_____

**Read Genesis 8:20-22. Identify both the decision maker and the circum-
stances surrounding his rededication.**

_____

How did God respond to his decision?

_____

**Confession of sin and rededication are found often in the New Testament.
Read John 21:15-17. How did Jesus restore the relationship between
Himself and Peter?**

_____

What was Peter's part in this event?

_____

Read Luke 24:54-62. Each person has had his own "rooster." Do you remember
a time when some event or circumstances reminded you of your unworthiness?
Take a moment to thank Jesus for His love and encouragement. Compose a short
prayer of thanksgiving in the space on page 74.

_____

_____

_____

Jesus encouraged Peter by trusting His "sheep" to Peter. As a decision counselor you are to be a source of encouragement to the person rededicating his life.

Jesus is not Lord of your life if you disobey Him. Read Luke 6:46-48.

What is the result of putting Jesus' words into practice in your life?

_____

Begin counseling for rededication by reading the opening paragraph of the Rededication to Grow Toward Christian Maturity panel. Follow the sequenced steps laid out in this section of the *Guide* given below.

You may feel you are not as close to Jesus as you once were, or you may realize you are not continuing to grow toward spiritual maturity.

God's Purpose

➤ Jesus wants to be Lord of all your life (Luke 6:46).
➤ God wants your life to be useful and joyful (John 15:10-11).
➤ God wants you to live in fellowship with Him (1 John 1:7).
➤ God wants to fill you with His Spirit (Eph. 5:18).
➤ God wants to equip you for ministry (2 Tim. 3:16-17).
➤ When you fail in your walk with Him, God wants to forgive you and restore you to a useful life with Him (1 John 1:9).

Read Luke 6:46. Ask the decision maker to read each statement of this section aloud. The Scripture reference can serve as an explanation if there are any questions or if the decision maker hesitates. Ask the decision maker to circle the phrase in each statement that identifies what God's wants. For now, circle these phrases in your *Guide*.

You should have circled "Lord of all your life," "useful and joyful," "live in fellowship with Him," "fill you with His Spirit," "equipped for ministry," and "forgive you and restore you." God's purpose for persons rededicating their lives to growing toward spiritual maturity can be summarized in the six statements of the "God's Purpose" section.

Tomorrow you will learn about a believer's need for spiritual transformation.

Day 2:
Spiritual Transformation

Above anything else, spiritual transformation is God's work. God creates a new identity in Christ in the new believer. Spiritual transformation describes a process in which God empowers the believer to grow in a relationship of love, trust, and obedience in Christ that glorifies God. A spiritually transformed person no longer conforms to the patterns of this world, but is transformed by the renewing of his mind in Christ (Rom. 12:2).

Spiritual transformation is the continuing process of being transformed into the likeness of Christ. A believer's spiritual transformation will include the decision to grow toward spiritual maturity.

In order to be in the process of spiritual transformation, a person must have a relationship with Christ. The end result of spiritual transformation is glorifying God.

Three Truths about Spiritual Transformation

1. Spiritual transformation begins with a new identity in Christ given by God at salvation. Read John 14:20.
2. Spiritual transformation is a growing relationship of love, trust, and obedience in Christ. Read Matthew 12:33.
3. Spiritual transformation ultimately glorifies God. Read John 15:8.

○ Circle the phrase that describes where spiritual transformation begins.

❐ Draw a box around the phrase that explains the continuing focus of spiritual transformation.

☆ Draw a star over the phrase that shows the ultimate result of spiritual transformation.

Read John 15:9. Once the transformational process has begun, love will become the heart of the believer. A decision to accept Christ as Lord and Savior begins the spiritual transformation process. A rededication to grow toward spiritual maturity can play a large part in the process of spiritual transformation. Encourage the decision maker to rejoice in God's role in her life.

Spiritual transformation begins with a new identity in Christ Jesus.

Believers are set apart, or sanctified, for God's purposes the moment they become a new creation in Christ. Salvation provides a new identity. When a person begins his journey of spiritual transformation he is a new creation (2 Cor. 5:17).

Read Romans 12:2. Copy this verse in the space below. Paying attention to each word, read this verse slowly to yourself.

_____

_____

_____

_____

Let these words speak to you. Imagine how God would speak to a decision maker through this verse. A desire for rededication is a means of renewal for the believer's mind.

Spiritual transformation continues in a growing relationship.

"Newly born" denotes a believer who is not fully mature in Christ. The work of the Holy Spirit continues to develop the fullness of the new identity believers have received by being in Christ. This is the very foundation of spiritual transformation. Believers will be reborn in Christ and continue to grow in the Spirit. Where would you place yourself if you had to compare your spiritual maturity to a physical age?

❏ Baby ❏ Toddler ❏ Child ❏ Teen ❏ Adult

The Holy Spirit brings a new perspective on world views, values, and behavior through spiritual transformation. When a believer decides to take another step forward in his walk with Christ, he will seek the next level of spiritual maturity.

True or false:

____ Spiritual transformation is an ongoing process.

____ The work of the Holy Spirit in a believer's life is over once the person accepts Jesus.

____ The decision for rededication is a sign of growing toward spiritual maturity.

(Answers: T, F, T)

Spiritual transformation glorifies God.

God is glorified through a love relationship with Christ. Not coincidentally, love is central to spiritual transformation.

Read John 13:33-34. How many times is love mentioned in this passage?

_____

Read John 15:8. What brings God glory?

_____

How will others know that we are disciples of Jesus?

_____

To know Jesus is to know the heart of God. Maintaining an intimate personal relationship with Jesus will transform a believer. Spiritual transformation leads to renewal. Through spiritual transformation a believer will change *from* thinking, seeing, feeling, and acting according to the pattern of the world, *to* thinking, seeing, feeling, and acting like Jesus. A believer who is being spiritually transformed will reflect the glory of God.

Inform the decision maker that spiritual transformation is a process that God desires to accomplish in each believer's life as you continue using the Rededication to Grow Toward Spiritual Maturity panel. Through the work of the Holy Spirit, God is transforming believers to be like Jesus and grow in a relationship of love, trust, and obedience that glorifies Him.

Our Need
➤ Personal sin may hinder our fellowship with God (Isa. 59:2).
➤ Circumstances of life may reveal a need for renewed or continuing growth toward maturity (Rom. 12:1-2).

Ask, Why would a believer seek rededication? Read the first statement of the section and Isaiah 59:2 aloud. Then, read the next statement and the accompanying Scripture passage. Explain the difference between a life that is centered on self and a life that is centered on Christ. Underline "living sacrifice," "Do not conform," and "transformed by the renewing of your mind."

God's Provision

God offers six major resources for transformation and spiritual growth.

➤ God uses Scripture to bring believers into a state of being set apart for His purposes (John 17:17).

➤ Spiritual disciplines, such as prayer, Bible study, worship, fasting, witnessing, and serving help us to grow (1 Tim. 4:7).

➤ Family and home influences may encourage us toward spiritual growth (2 Tim. 1:5).

➤ The church, as the body of Christ, encourages all to reach unity in their faith and knowledge of Jesus (Eph. 4:12-13).

➤ God works in all circumstances of life to bring us to Christlikeness (Rom. 8:28-29).

➤ God disciplines His children to transform us into the likeness of Jesus (Heb. 12:10).

The "God's Provision" section emphasizes God's readiness to accept a person's rededication. Tell the decision maker that there are six major resources for transformation and spiritual growth. Read the six statements. Scripture references are provided to answer any questions a decision maker may have. Summarize "God's Provision" with these statements:

- God is ready to forgive you.
- Jesus has already paid the price for your sins.
- Other Christians will love and support you.

Encourage the believer by making the above statements clear. Tomorrow your study will focus on how to grow toward spiritual maturity.

Day 3:
God Enables Us to Grow

Read 2 Corinthians 3:18. According to Paul, we are being transformed into the likeness of Jesus. This isn't something we do for ourselves; it is God's work in us and it is ongoing.

Paraphrase 2 Corinthians 3:18 in the space below.

_____

_____

_____

In Galatians 2:20, Paul says that he has been "crucified with Christ." The moment we accept Christ as our Lord and Savior the old is gone. Transformation into the likeness of Christ begins for every believer at the moment of salvation. We are able to grow in spiritual maturity because of our relationship with God. Spiritual transformation cannot occur apart from our relationship with God. To be transformed a person must approach God with a clear heart. Transformation is possible only by justification through faith.

A Relationship of Love, Trust, and Obedience with Jesus

At the foundation of spiritual transformation is a change of heart so profound that it manifests itself in the outward life of a believer. Believers are transformed from inside out. Christians will desire to rededicate their lives to the lordship of Christ as the Holy Spirit defines with increasing clarity the disparity between loving Jesus and loving the material world. Feeling and acknowledging the disparity between Christ and the world is among the first steps toward spiritual maturity.

As you learned in yesterday's study of the "God's Provision" section of the *Guide*, the Holy Spirit uses different agents to facilitate spiritual transformation: Scripture, spiritual exercises for godliness, family, people, circumstances, and God's discipline. Today, we will examine each of these resources more extensively.

Scripture. Growth toward spiritual maturity cannot happen apart from Scripture. Bible study and Scripture memory are both conditions for growth. As a counselor you will want to encourage the believer who desires to grow toward spiritual maturity to study God's Word on a regular basis.

As mentioned in Week 1, growth is a characteristic of a decision counselor. If you are not studying the Bible on a regular basis, now is a good time to commit a portion of your day every day to grow toward spiritual maturity through a study of Scripture.

I will commit to:

_____

Spiritual Exercises for Godliness. In order for us to be open to God's work we must seek His counsel. In 1 Timothy 4:7 Paul tells us to train ourselves to be godly. Spiritual disciplines are the means by which we place ourselves in the presence of God for this training. These disciplines include prayer, Bible study, fasting, worship, evangelism, service, stewardship, and education. Use the margin to identify the disciplines in which you place yourself for godly training.

Spending a portion of each day with God in prayer, meditation, and Bible study does not happen by chance. Here are some tips for establishing consistent and effective spiritual exercises:
➤ Make this time the first time of your day.
➤ Have an established and predetermined time and place.
➤ Develop a plan for Bible study, prayer, and meditation. Journaling is also a wonderful habit to develop and cultivate.

Family. God uses parents and other family members as instruments of spiritual growth.

The Church. The body of Christ functions together so all will reach unity in their faith and knowledge of Jesus. Just like the prophets, there are those open to God's call who are used as a mouthpiece by God. Prayerfully listen to the words of men and women of God.

Circumstances. Scripture teaches us that God uses everything to work for the good of those who love Him and have been called according to His purpose (Rom. 8:28). Be aware of the work going on around you. Being sensitive to circumstances is being sensitive to the activity of God Himself.

God's Discipline. God disciplines His children to make us holy and to transform us into the likeness of Christ. Throughout the Old Testament God uses judgment as a companion to restoration and renewal. In the New Testament, Jesus claims that His grace is sufficient for us (2 Cor. 12:9). God's discipline prompts us to seek Him.

Circle the agents above that God has used in your life recently.

Briefly describe God's use of the agent(s) in your life.

_____

_____

_____

_____

There are three basic responses involved in rededication. These responses are represented in the acrostic C.R.Y.

Confession of sin involves more than simply saying, "Forgive me if I have sinned." It means agreeing with God that specific acts and attitudes are contrary to God's way.

Recommitment to the lordship of Christ means giving Him control of your life as you ask Him to direct your attitudes and activities.

Yielding to Jesus must be a daily experience as you grow toward the fullness of the life He wants you to have.

Our Response

➤ Confess any known sin (Prov. 28:13).
➤ Recommit your life to the lordship of Jesus Christ (John 20:28).
➤ Yield yourself daily to Jesus and experience the fullness of His life in you as you continually grow toward spiritual maturity (Rom. 6:12-13; Gal. 2:20).

A decision maker must be prepared for God's continued guidance. To be open, believers must know what agents God uses to speak. Continue the counseling session with the "Our Response" section of this panel. Review the C.R.Y. acrostic with the decision maker: Confession of sin, Recommitment to the lordship of Christ, and Yielding daily to Christ and experiencing the fullness of His life within. You should have time to read the referenced Scripture passages for each point of C.R.Y.

Tomorrow you will learn what a decision maker should expect as he is transformed into the likeness of Christ.

Day 4:
Evidence of Spiritual Growth

Discipleship is measured by the degree to which a believer is like Jesus. Character-based transformation reveals an inner Christlikeness evidenced by the fruit of the Spirit. Pray that God will continue to develop the fruit of His Spirit in your life.

Read Galatians 5:22-23. The fruit is the product of the Holy Spirit's transforming work in the life of the believer. Identify the fruit of the Spirit in the margin. Circle the words that you feel have the strongest presence in your life.

It is important for you and the decision maker to realize that transformation doesn't focus on the believer completing growth activities and isn't activity based. Transformation is the result of the inner spiritual growth that comes from loving, trusting, and obeying Jesus. Spiritual growth is initiated by the Holy Spirit's work in the life of a person and completed by the eternal union of a believer with Christ.

Characteristics of a Christian Growing Toward Spiritual Maturity

The believer is characterized by love. A believer growing toward spiritual maturity knows the heart of Christ. A believer characterized by love follows Him, obeys Him, and is characterized by His love. Jesus wants everyone to have what He has (John 16:13-15). The spiritually maturing Christian will want to share Christ with everyone through love. **Read John 17:24 and summarize Jesus' prayer for believers in the space here.**

_____

The believer lives in harmony with God's Word. The outward evidence of inner spiritual transformation is manifested by living consistently with the teachings of Jesus and God's Word. Living harmoniously with God's Word will bear the fruit referred to in Galatians 5:22-23. **According to Matthew 12:33, by what can we judge a person's spiritual growth?**

_____

The believer sees the world through a scriptural lens. Colossians 3:2 reads, "Set your minds on things above, not earthly things." Allowing the world we see to be colored by the Bible is one way we can set our minds on things above. **How are we to transcend this world and move toward spiritual maturity?**

The believer serves through the church. A believer should minister as a member of the body of Christ to build the church. The Spirit of God dispenses spiritual gifts to help believers fulfill this purpose. Ephesians 4:11 informs us, "It was he who gave some to be apostles, some to be prophets, some to be evangelists, and some to be pastors and teachers." Other gifts mentioned in the Bible are leadership, discernment, exhortation, shepherding, service, and giving. **Identify the spiritual gift or gifts that may have led you to become a decision counselor.**

_____

_____

The believer proclaims God's love. As individuals and as a part of the body of Christ, the believer is to fulfill God's purpose: to proclaim the good news of salvation through faith in Christ.

Read John 17:2. What did Jesus come to do?

_____

_____

Read John 17:18. Jesus has sent us into the world just as He was sent into the world. What is the role of the believer in the world?

_____

_____

How do you see decision counseling fulfilling the work of the believer in the world?

_____

_____

My Commitment

As you respond to God's call to growth, you will begin to see the fruit of the Spirit being developed in your life (Gal. 5:22-23).

Perhaps you can identify one or more aspects of the fruit of the Spirit which are lacking in your life. Are you ready to ask God to work in you to help you grow toward the fullness of His life? If so, you may want to pray the following prayer or a similar one:

"Heavenly Father, I want to be like Jesus. I commit myself to you and ask you to work in my life to develop the fruit of the Spirit so I may become continually more mature in my faith."

After the "Our Response" section, move to the "My Commitment" section of the Rededication to Grow Toward Christian Maturity panel.

Spiritual maturity is the result of our relationship with Jesus. True spiritual transformation is inner spiritual growth based on love, trust, and obedience in Christ. It is the work of God's Spirit that transforms us into the likeness of Christ.

Read the first paragraph of "My Commitment." After reading the passage from Galatians, point out that the fruit of the Spirit is a product of a growing relationship with Jesus. If the decision maker agrees, read the next statement and the question that follows. Once the decision maker affirms his decision, close the session by praying the prayer of commitment given at the bottom of the panel. Be sure the decision maker receives information on discipleship experiences that are available in your church.

After completing and detaching the Commitment Record, give the rest of the *Guide* to the decision maker as a reference.

Pray for your own spiritual transformation and the work that the Spirit of God is doing in your life. Tomorrow you will take a closer look at some barriers to spiritual transformation.

Day 5:
Barriers to Spiritual Growth

"Finally, be strong in the Lord and in his mighty power. Put on the full armor of God so that you can take your stand against the devil's schemes. For our struggle is not against flesh and blood, but against the rulers, against the authorities, against the powers of this dark world and against the spiritual forces of evil in the heavenly realms" (Eph. 6:10-13).

What is the purpose of putting on physical armor in a battle?

_____

_____

Read 1 Peter 5:8. As a decision counselor, you may want to bring these verses to the decision maker's attention. Satan will be trying to thwart the decision maker's attempt to grow in Christ. **How can this verse help the decision maker as this rededication is made?**

_____

_____

Believers need to be aware of the barriers to Christlikeness. These barriers will hinder a believer's growth in Christ and become an obstacle to the transforming power of the Holy Spirit. Here are some barriers to spiritual transformation:

Desires of the flesh. The old nature of self-centeredness engages the believer in a spiritual war against being God-centered. **According to Galatians 5:17, what does a sinful nature desire?**

_____

Lack of faith. Lack of trust in Jesus as Lord of everything is an enormous barrier to spiritual growth. **Read John 14:1. Referring to this verse, how can believers avoid being troubled?**

_____

Satan. Ephesians 6:10-11, "Finally, be strong in the Lord and in his mighty power. Put on the full armor of God so that you can take your stand against the devil's schemes."

Even though the ultimate victory has been won by Christ, we face a perpetual battle against the evil one. A believer should never underestimate the enemy's interest in being a barrier to spiritual growth.

The World. A believer constantly faces temptation to conform to the world's perspective and its way of doing things. The love of God cannot dwell in the same heart that loves the material world (1 John 2:15).

Drifting. "Drifting," as opposed to rebellion, is a gradual loss of focus on spiritual matters. Generally, a believer does not drift deliberately. Many times other barriers will contribute to drifting. Once a believer falls out of sorts with the heart of God, he no longer has a foundation, or anchor for his spiritual growth.

Rebellion. A deliberate turning away from God and spiritual concerns is called "rebellion." Whereas drifting is a lack of effort and therefore passive, rebellion is a conscious effort and therefore active. "They stumble because they disobey the message" (1 Pet. 2:8). Rebellious disobedience causes a believer to stumble or fall.

Lack of knowledge. A lack of scriptural knowledge may lead to an unawareness of the new identity and power a person possesses in Christ. Where will this knowledge be found? Knowledge can be obtained through daily Bible reading. Read 2 Timothy 3:14-17. During the counseling session you may want to discuss with the decision maker the importance of daily personal Bible study and group Bible study and discipleship opportunities.

Distraction. Distraction is perhaps the most effective barrier to spiritual growth used by Satan. Activities, fears, failures, personal ambition, and the world around us can cause our eyes to stray away from our relationship with Jesus and spiritual concerns.

Identify problems in your life which create barriers to spiritual growth.

_____

Read 1 John 5:14-15. Write a prayer of commitment asking God to strengthen you against those barriers.

_____

_____

Week 6

Distinct Counseling Situations

This week you will recognize distinct counseling situations and learn skills helpful for counseling decision makers in these situations.

Day 1:
Understanding Children

God's purpose, our need, God's provision, and our response remain the same for those making decisions—regardless of the age of the decision maker. There is only one plan of salvation.

Because of their level of understanding, children must be counseled in language that they can understand. In this case, a child is anyone who may not have the mental attributes and the emotional capabilities to understand fully the significance of a decision of this nature.

Children may respond to an invitation for reasons other than repentance and salvation. Wanting to be like friends; wanting to participate in the Lord's Supper; and wanting to please adults are all possible motivations for responding to an invitation. Although a decision counselor will want to use language a child can understand, don't manipulate a session to such a degree that would allow a decision to be made that is not based on repentance for salvation.

God has a different plan of salvation for children.   ☐ Agree   ☐ Disagree

What the Bible Teaches
Read Matthew 18:1-14, Matthew 19:13-15, and Mark 10:13-16.
Did Jesus take the ministry to children seriously?   ☐ Yes ☐ No
Referring to these verses, did Jesus turn any children away?   ☐ Yes ☐ No

God wants His children to be saved. These passages not only show us how the Father feels, but also show us how important children are to Jesus. Jesus often called attention to children in order to teach great truths.

Return to Matthew 19:14. Why did Jesus tell the disciples to let the children come to Him?

_____

_____

Jesus said, " 'The kingdom of heaven belongs to such as these' " (Matt. 19:14). Because a child can have the faith and trust necessary to receive Christ as Savior, we should minister to them as Jesus did. Jesus was never overly concerned with a person's age. Even if a child has yet to come into an understanding of salvation, your words as a counselor may have an eternal impact. Don't attempt to put limits on the power of the Holy Spirit. Don't forget that we can do all things through Christ.

Age of Accountability

Since children mature at different ages, there is no certain age for accountability. Be it a matter of maturity, relationships, or exposure to the gospel, some children are too young to repent of sin and make a faith commitment to Christ. But this doesn't mean that we take a child's decision any less seriously. A child can have the faith necessary to accept Christ as Savior.

The following points regarding a child's potential for accountability give counselors a good base of understanding in this matter:

1. Trying to understand that accountability is far more important than trying to determine a specific age at which a child may be judged as lost.
2. The age at which any one child reaches accountability may vary rather immensely from the age at which another child reaches accountability.
3. Watering down biblical teachings about conversion so a child can respond affirmatively to Christ is a dangerous practice. Outside of simplifying the language, make no exceptions to the *Personal Commitment Guide*.
4. Respect the work of the Holy Spirit in the conversion of children.
5. One must respect a child's capacities, neither overrating nor underrating them.
6. Although it is accepted that a child may not be able to express his inner life in adult language or experiences, basic truths cannot be simplified or reduced.

Pray for wisdom and discernment when you counsel a child who has come forward.

Day 2:
Counseling Children

Special considerations must be made when counseling a child for a conversion decision. Use the following tips as guidelines to use in conjunction with the *Personal Commitment Guide*.

Use Open-Ended Questions

Children can often repeat words or use them correctly without actually comprehending their meaning. Because of this, a decision counselor should avoid questions with a "built in" answer or those that can be answered with a "yes" or "no." Instead, ask open-ended questions. Insert these open-ended questions when counseling children:

- Why have you come forward?
- Why do you want to become a Christian?
- Has something happened lately that has made you think about Jesus?
- Why do you think a person needs to become a Christian?
- What is sin?

Listen Closely

Children need to ask questions and have time to think and respond to your questions. Listening closely will allow you to detect a child's possible motivation for responding to the invitation. Use the Better Listening Strategies given in Week 1. Because children often respond because of friends, parents, baptism, or the Lord's Supper, clarifying the child's motivation could prove helpful.

Give Your Undivided Attention

A child can sense if you are genuinely interested in him. Put yourself at a child's eye level. If a child is accompanied by an adult, be sure to give your attention and direct your questions to the child—not the adult.

Use the Bible and the *Personal Commitment Guide*

Follow the *Personal Commitment Guide* when counseling for salvation. Help the child understand difficult words. Do not use any Scripture in addition to what is given in the *Guide*.

Make the Presentation Brief

Children have short attention spans. Do not give more information than a child is ready to receive. Bring the counseling session to an end if the child loses interest in the conversation or seems to have trouble understanding. Let them know that someone will be available if they would like to discuss the decision another time.

Use Language the Child Can Understand

The basic truths of the gospel and God's plan for salvation must be told on a child's level of understanding. Simplifying is not watering down. So, take time to explain words that the child may not know. The Holy Spirit speaks a language even a child can understand. You can't turn a person away from counseling because of a limited vocabulary.

Explaining salvation is not an easy task. Using the margin, take a few minutes to compose simplified explanations for the following words: "accept Jesus as Savior," "lost," "commit your life," "saved," "come forward," "give your heart," and "profession of faith."

You will be using the *Guide* as you counsel a child for salvation. Some terms in the *Guide* have to be explained to an adult, so you can imagine why explanation would be even more appropriate if counseling a child. In the right column below are simplified expressions for the terms on the left.

World . . . . All people
Believe/Faith . . . . Trust completely
Perish . . . . Die and be separated from God forever
Sin . . . . Choosing your way instead of God's way or doing things that do not please God
Eternal Life . . . . Never ending life with Jesus
Repent . . . . Turn away from the wrong things you have done and obey Jesus

Depend on the Holy Spirit

Above all else, know that you can trust the Holy Spirit to bring conviction and understanding to any decision maker He has called. Remember, God loves this child more than you ever could.

Pray with the Child

At the end of the counseling session, ask the child, "Do you want to trust Jesus as your Savior right now, or wait?" If she would like to trust Jesus as her Lord and Savior, then continue in prayer. Tell her that prayer is talking with God.

First, pray for the child. Assure her that God knows her feelings as she prays. You might paraphrase the prayer of commitment in the Salvation panel. If you do, let the child repeat each phrase after you.

Follow Up

At the end of the counseling time, let the child know that the pastor, another church staff member, or a children's leader will make an appointment for the follow up talk with the child and parents.

Practice: Write a paraphrase of these Scriptures in language that can be understood by a child.

Romans 3:23:

_____

_____

John 3:16:

_____

_____

Day 3:
Counseling for Vocational Christian Ministry

Every Christian is called to minister. The Bible is clear in its teaching that all believers have responsibility for ministry. **As believers, what ministry have we been given by God? (Find 2 Corinthians 5:17-21 for the answer.)**

Paraphrase 1 Peter 2:9 in the space below.

According to this verse, every believer is a priest. This New Testament doctrine identifies two characteristics for believers:
- Each believer has direct access to God.
- Each believer is to minister so that others may come to know God.

In Ephesians 4:11-12 Paul tells believers that they have been gifted for works of service. Read this verse and list some of the examples of service.

These examples of service are important and relate specifically to persons who indicate a desire to enter a vocational Christian ministry. But God has called all of us to the ministry of reconciliation. We don't have to be apostles, prophets, evangelists, or pastors to be considered ministers. As believers, we are all ministers.

Why is it important for the person making a decision for vocational Christian ministry to realize that every believer is called to minister?

Persons who come forward for vocational ministry are seeking meaning and fulfillment. They desire to be actively involved as a minister of Jesus Christ. It is a mistaken idea to believe the only way they can truly serve God is through Christian vocation.

Some persons are called to serve in an equipping ministry. Equipping ministry helps other believers fulfill their ministry. For instance, a Sunday School worker will provide students with a lesson to help them fulfill their ministry in the workplace. A pastor equips his congregation for service in the body of Christ. Equipping ministry is not a call to raise some believers to a higher relationship with God than others. Ephesians 4:16 claims that each part of the church is held together by every other part. Equipping ministry is the essence of the body of Christ.

Use the Commitment to Vocational Christian Ministry panel of the *Guide* when counseling persons making a decision for vocational Christian service. Begin by asking the decision maker the opening question. Read Ephesians 5:17, Romans 12:2, and the statement that follows the question. Read the introductory statement in this section. Ask the decision maker the opening question.

> What do you think God wants you to do with your life? God wants you to know His will (Eph. 5:17), and He will help you discover it (Rom. 12:2).

Use the space below to answer this question yourself.

_____

_____

_____

_____

Make it clear to the decision maker that the first statement supports the "kingdom of priests" principle (Ex. 19:6, 1 Pet. 2:9). This principle maintains that all of God's people are to be ministers. Read each of the four statements and the supporting Scripture verses given under "God's Purpose." Ask the decision maker to read Ephesians 4:11-12 aloud. Let the decision

God's Purpose
➤ Every Christian is called to ministry, that is, to Christian service (Eph. 4:1).
➤ God reaches out through His people to the world (2 Cor. 5:20).
➤ God gives us spiritual gifts to minister to others (Rom. 12:6, 1 Pet. 4:10).
➤ God gives leaders to the church to equip its people for ministry: "It was he who gave some to be apostles, some to be prophets, some to be evangelists, and some to be pastors and teachers, to prepare God's people for works of service, so that the body of Christ may be built up" (Eph. 4:11-12).

Our Need
➤ We need to be laborers in the fields that are ready for harvest (Luke 10:2).
➤ We need to sense an urgency of sharing the gospel because so many in the world are lost and headed for eternity in hell (Matt. 7:13).
➤ We need to obey the will of God as He reveals it. "For it is God who works in you to will and to act according to his good purpose" (Phil. 2:13).
➤ We need to equip others for service (2 Tim. 2:2).

maker know that there are many directions that vocational Christian ministry can take today.

The first statement of the "Our Need" section stresses the significance of a commitment to vocational Christian ministry. A person accepting God's call to Christian vocation must also accept the immediacy of God's charge. The second statement suggests the urgency involved when doing God's work.

Read the Scripture passages that accompany the first two statements. Allow a moment for the decision maker to respond. Continue by reading the third statement of this section and Philippians 2:13. Ask the decision maker to read the last statement aloud. Circle "laborers in the fields," "urgency of sharing the gospel," "will of God," and "equip others" as you counsel. Ask the decision maker to read 2 Timothy 2:2 aloud before addressing God's provision.

The "God's Provision" section identifies the ways God prepares and equips a person for vocational service. Read each statement of this section. Use the Scripture verses to answer any questions the decision maker may ask.

God's Provision
➤ God will equip you for the ministry He gives you (Phil. 2:13).
➤ It is God who calls you to Christian service (1 Sam. 3:8-9; Acts 9:1-20).
➤ God promises to be with you and to strengthen you (Ex. 4:12; Josh. 1:9).
➤ The Holy Spirit will empower you (Acts 1:8).
➤ Anything He leads you to do is possible in His strength: "I can do everything through him who gives me strength" (Phil. 4:13).

Ask the decision maker to underline the words *God* and *Holy Spirit*. Stress that the call to vocational ministry and the results of such service all come from God. Even though He doesn't need our help, a merciful and loving God invites believers to become involved with Him in His work.

A reading of Romans 12:1-2 will illustrate for the decision maker how best to respond to God's call. Write "living sacrifice" beside the first point in the copy to the right. Ask the decision maker to do this during counseling. Read the second statement and then read Luke 5:5. Ask the decision maker to read Proverbs 3:5-6 first silently to herself, and then aloud. This passage from Proverbs will help the decision maker identify ways to discover and follow God's will. Make these practical suggestions to help the decision maker discover God's will:

- Ask yourself, "Am I willing to do God's will?"
- Seek the counsel of other committed Christians.
- Pray for specific guidance.
- Stay in daily contact with God through His Word.
- Describe God's call in writing when you get home.

Ask the first question in "My Commitment." If the answer is "No," pray for God's guidance in the decision maker's life. If the response is "Yes," continue. Ask the second question to reaffirm the decision maker's commitment. In your Bible find Matthew 25:21 and 1 Corinthians 4:2 for the decision maker. Ask him to read these verses aloud. Read the next two statements and circle "serve," "faithfully," "commit," and "God's will." Lead the decision maker in the prayer of commitment.

After completing and detaching the Commitment Record, give the *Guide* to the decision maker as a reference. Your church might also want to have copies of *God's Call: The Cornerstone of Effective Ministry* available to give to the person making a commitment to a vocational Christian ministry. (See page 100 for ordering information.)

Our Response
➤ Discover God's will for service by complete surrender to Jesus as Lord (Rom. 12:1-2).
➤ Commit yourself to doing what God directs you to do (Luke 5:5; 9:23).
➤ Trust God for guidance. "Trust in the Lord with all your heart and lean not on your own understanding; in all your ways acknowledge him, and he will make your paths straight" (Prov. 3:5-6).

My Commitment
Are you willing to do God's will? If you are, He will reveal His will to you, a step at a time.

Will you respond to each step as God reveals it and trust Him for the next steps?

Your first step is to serve faithfully where you are (Matt. 25:21; 1 Cor. 4:2).

If you are willing to commit yourself to following God's will for all of your life, you may want to pray the following or a similar prayer:

"Dear Lord, thank you for providing a perfect plan for my life. I am committed to obeying your will as you reveal it to me."

Day 4:
Referring Persons with Special Problems

Many people seeking spiritual counsel have problems that are too involved—too emotional, too severe, or too intimate—for a decision counselor to handle. Your task as a counselor is not to give advice, but to provide spiritual support through prayer, proclamation of God's love, and effective counseling. As is the case in most counseling situations, confidentiality is very important.

If you sense that a decision or special problem requires training beyond yours, use an indirect counseling approach. A decision counselor using this approach will ask open-ended questions designed to avoid specifics such as "How do you feel led by God?" or "What are you feeling?"

Persons with Moral and Ethical Problems

Decisions that are the result of drug abuse, alcoholism, child abuse, premarital sex, homosexuality, failing or failed relationships, and family conflicts are common problems. As has already been stated, your ministry should be supportive but not advisory. Follow these guidelines:

- Assure the decision maker of God's love and forgiveness.
- Assure the decision maker that there is no problem that God cannot handle.

What assurance did Jesus give all believers in Matthew 19:26?

_____

- Express spiritual compassion and sensitivity.
- Be positive rather than judgmental. Do not react with shock, reproof, or anger.
- Communicate that God forgives sin when a person is repentant and confesses the sin. **What is the message in 1 John 1:9?**

_____

_____

- If appropriate, lead the decision maker in seeking God's forgiveness. Explain that Jesus paid the price so that feeling guilty is not necessary.

Paraphrase Romans 8:38-39.

_____

_____

Persons with Psychological Problems

Some people's lives are complicated with psychological problems such as depression; personality and eating disorders; suicidal tendencies; and anxiety. These problems are beyond the scope of a decision counselor's role in the service. If such a person comes forward during the invitation for help, it is best to listen, pray, and refer him to the pastor.

Follow-Up

Encourage the decision maker to seek pastoral or other professional counseling in dealing with the moral, ethical, or psychological problem. Ask for the decision maker's permission to contact the pastor about the problem. Individuals displaying psychological problems need the guidance of a trained professional. When completing the Personal Commitment Card, do not write in any personal information. Simply write "Needs further counseling" just outside of the box marked "Other."

The first step in the follow-up process in these cases is the pastor. The pastor may refer them to other Christian professionals.

Day 5:
Providing Follow-Up

Today's study will focus on the follow-up process in greater detail. Your church's follow-up ministry is vital to God's Kingdom.

Initial Follow-Up

Initial follow-up should begin immediately after a new Christian's prayer of commitment. The first step in this follow-up is completing the Commitment Record. This card will link the new Christian to the church and its follow-up ministry.

Completion of the Commitment Record is followed by a brief summary of two other panels: Baptism and Church Membership. Give the decision maker a tract welcoming him to the family of God and close in prayer.

New church members can join the fellowship in basically three ways:

1. Profession of faith in Jesus followed by baptism.
2. Transfer of church membership from one Baptist church to another Baptist church of like beliefs and practices.
3. Statement that the member is a Christian and has been baptized by immersion by a church of like beliefs and practices.

Circle the words that identify the three traditional ways a person can join a Baptist church. You should have circled "profession," "transfer," and "statement."

New believers should be offered a plan of encouragement after a conversion experience. This plan usually affords new Christians an opportunity to learn the basic steps for living a Christian life from a mature Christian. See page 100 for possible follow-up resources for the decision maker.

Immediate Follow-Up

A home visit should be made within the week. The church needs to have a process for this follow-up visit. Usually the decision counselor is not the person expected to make this visit.

Information about church ministries, the church calendar, and other important information can be given during this visit. But most of all, this visit is to welcome the decision maker into your church, invite him to services and Sunday School, and answer any questions.

All new members need to complete the church's new member follow-up plan. This can be completed individually or as a member of a group. Many churches conduct an ongoing new member class.

Sunday School

Every new Christian and every other new church member must be enrolled in a Sunday School class. This is where fellowship and foundational discipleship is experienced.

Discipleship Experiences

All believers need to have opportunities for continued growth toward spiritual maturity. Every person making a decision should be encouraged to participate in discipleship experiences.

Reflect: Now that you are completing *DecisionTime: Commitment Counseling,* **how would you describe the work of a decision counselor?**

_____

_____

   Congratulations! You have finished this six-week preparation for decision counseling. You now have the God-given opportunity and privilege to counsel persons and help them as they make life-changing decisions. Pray for guidance as you fulfill the role of decision counselor.

Follow-up Resources for Decision Makers

The decision maker will need a lot of help as he or she begins this new journey of faith. You may wish to suggest several resources which will help.

Welcome to God's Family.—This pocket-sized tract utilizes Scripture verses, drawings, and brief comments to provide guidance and positive reinforcement to those who have recently accepted Jesus as Savior. It will also help them establish new habits of discipleship and will encourage them to join the fellowship of the church. This tract will give new Christians the immediate guidance they need upon a profession of faith.

Beginning Steps: A Seven-Day Growth Guide for New Believers.—This simple seven-step booklet can guide a new Christian during the crucial first week after becoming a believer.

Taking the Next Step: A Guide for New Church Members.—This easy-to-use interactive resource will help new members find their place in God's work through your church. It provides an overview and orientation for assimilation of new church members, and guides them toward meaningful involvement in your church's life and ministry.

Survival Kit for Christians.—This six-week study will help adults who are new Christians to develop a regular pattern of quiet time, prayer, Bible study, and Scripture memory.

Survival Kit for Youth, Revised.—Helps youth who are new Christians to understand the basics of a growing faith, complete with ways to get into a consistent lifestyle of quiet time, prayer, Bible study, and Scripture memory.

Survival Kit for New Christians, Children's Edition.—This resource provides a six-week study guide for older children who are new Christians to use at home five days per week. It also includes Scripture cards to encourage Scripture memory.

Now That I'm a Christian, Revised Edition.—This easy-to-understand guide will help children understand what it means to be a Christian. It is designed to be used by children with the help of a parent or other adult.

God's Call: The Cornerstone of Effective Ministry.—This three-chapter interactive study helps an individual work through his or her sense of call to a vocational Christian ministry.

To order additional copies of these resources: WRITE LifeWay Church Resources Customer Service; One LifeWay Plaza; Nashville, TN 37234-0113; FAX order to (615) 251-5933; PHONE (800) 458-2772; EMAIL to *customerservice@lifeway.com*; ORDER ONLINE at *www.lifeway.com*; or VISIT the LifeWay Christian Store serving you.

Follow-up Resources for Commitment Counselors

You will want to become familiar with the follow-up resources that you might be suggesting for decision makers. However, the following resources are suggested as possible next steps as you continue your exciting journey of maturing in Christ. Each of these resources may be studied individually, or you may wish to ask your pastor, other church ministers, or discipleship director about the possibility of scheduling a small-group study soon.

Share Jesus Without Fear.—This resource presents a natural, non-threatening way to share the gospel that eliminates the pressure, the argument, and the fear of failure. There is no personal rejection, no argument, and no failure. The goal is simply to share your faith, allowing the Holy Spirit to do the convicting, the convincing, and the teaching through His own Word.

In God's Presence: Your Daily Guide to a Meaningful Prayer Life.—Develop a meaningful, faithful prayer life with this simple, interactive book. Readers will learn about and practice six types of prayer and will discover the greater authority granted to united prayer.

Experiencing God: Knowing and Doing the Will of God.—This popular resource helps Christians discover God's will and obediently follow it. Daily learning and devotional activities help participants develop an intimate relationship with God so that they can hear when God is speaking. It also leads participants to reorganize their beliefs, character, and behavior around God's will.

Jesus on Leadership: Becoming a Servant Leader.—In too many churches today, head tables have replaced the towel and washbasin as symbols of leadership among God's people. *Jesus on Leadership* will guide the reader to stop following the world's model for leadership and adopt Jesus' teachings. This resource presents the true meaning of biblical servant leadership.

MasterLife: A Biblical Process for Growing Disciples.—*MasterLife* provides a small-group discipling process that guides believers to develop a lifelong, obedient relationship with Jesus Christ. As believers learn to practice six biblical disciplines, they become more Christlike, develop Kingdom values, and become involved in His mission in the home, the church, and the world.

Meeting Needs: Sharing Christ: Ministry Evangelism in Today's New Testament Church.—This book leads church members to understand the concept and capture the vision for ministry evangelism. It will help readers see the church's purpose for ministry evangelism; identify ministry needs in their community; and discover ways to minister to broken lives.

Life in the Spirit.—Readers will discover a special quality of life, a life characterized by a deep and loving relationship with God, effectiveness in personal living, and ministry that makes a difference in the world.

See page 100 for ordering information.

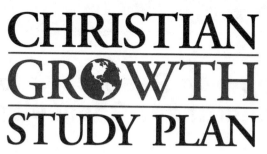

CHRISTIAN GROWTH STUDY PLAN

Preparing Christians to Serve

102

In the **Christian Growth Study Plan (formerly Church Study Course),** this book *DecisionTime: Commitment Counseling* is a resource for course credit in the subject area Evangelism of the Christian Growth category of plans. To receive credit, read the book, complete the learning activities, show your work to your pastor, a staff member or church leader, then complete the following information. This page may be duplicated. Send the completed page to:

Christian Growth Study Plan
• One LifeWay Plaza • Nashville, TN 37234-0117
• FAX: (615)251-5067 • Email: cgspnet@lifeway.com
For information about the Christian Growth Study Plan, refer to the Christian Growth Study Plan Catalog. It is located online at *www.lifeway.com/cgsp.* If you do not have access to the Internet, contact the Christian Growth Study Plan office (1.800.968.5519) for the specific plan you need for your ministry.

DecisionTime: Commitment Counseling
Course Number CG-0078

PARTICIPANT INFORMATION

Social Security Number (USA ONLY-optional)   Personal CGSP Number*   Date of Birth (MONTH, DAY, YEAR)

Name (First, Middle, Last)   Home Phone

Address (Street, Route, or P.O. Box)   City, State, or Province   Zip/Postal Code

Please check appropriate box: ❏ Resource purchased by self ❏ Resource purchased by church ❏ Other

CHURCH INFORMATION

Church Name

Address (Street, Route, or P.O. Box)   City, State, or Province   Zip/Postal Code

CHANGE REQUEST ONLY

❏ Former Name

❏ Former Address   City, State, or Province   Zip/Postal Code

❏ Former Church   City, State, or Province   Zip/Postal Code

Signature of Pastor, Conference Leader, or Other Church Leader   Date

*New participants are requested but not required to give SS# and date of birth. Existing participants, please give CGSP# when using SS# for the first time.
Thereafter, only one ID# is required. **Mail to:** Christian Growth Study Plan, One LifeWay Plaza, Nashville, TN 37234-0117. Fax: (615)251-5067.

Rev. 3-03

Facilitator's Guide

DECISIONTIME: COMMITMENT COUNSELING

Before You Begin Leading *DecisionTime*

The Purpose of This Study

Because ministry is everyone's responsibility, members can help pastors and other church staff meet the critical needs of the church. One of those needs is counseling new believers, persons desiring to become church members, and others making spiritual decisions. *DecisionTime: Commitment Counseling* has been written for church members who have felt the call to assist in a decision counseling ministry. The trained decision counselors also may serve the community of believers during area crusades, rallies, youth and children's camps, evangelism conferences, or any other time public invitations are given.

Every church needs a group of dedicated and trained decision counselors for these reasons:

1. To make sure the person trusts Jesus,
2. To clarify the decision being made,
3. To encourage those making decisions,
4. To help when several persons respond to the invitation, and
5. To maintain accurate records for follow-up.

DecisionTime requires commitment. Because kingdom work is a responsibility to be taken seriously, you must remain faithful in your commitment to lead this group. Cultivating relationships, growing in Christ, and leading people to Jesus are some of the benefits of leading and completing a course of this nature. Set aside a daily prayer time during which you ask for God's guidance. Also pray for participants as they work to complete *DecisionTime.* Enjoy bringing glory to your Lord and Savior.

Decision Counseling Team

Look on pages 6-7 for the seven functions for the decision counseling team. Determine who will be responsible for the six functions other than decision counselor. As few as two people can handle these six functions (such as the pastor also serving as receiver and presenter and the coordinator also serving as the trainer and advisor). Write the names of the person who will be responsible for each function here:

Pastor _____

Coordinator _____

Trainer_____

Receiver_____

Advisor _____

Presenter_____

Personal Commitment Guide

The *Personal Commitment Guide* is a folder that outlines the decision counseling process for six different types of decisions and includes a Commitment Record. You will need one *Guide* for each person who will make a decision. At the conclusion of the commitment counseling time, the decision counselor will tearing off the perforated Commitment Record and give the rest of the *Guide* to the decision maker.

Commitment Counseling Room

Decision counseling will need a separate room or area from the reception area in the worship center. Although some churches will find it necessary to use the reception area as the counseling area, this should be done only if no other space is available. Having a separate room keeps the reception area open for others coming to make decisions, allows for better privacy, and provides a more relaxed atmosphere for conversation between the counselor and decision maker, and reduces distractions.

The counseling room should be a clean, fresh, and bright room easily accessed from the worship center. Create an atmosphere that is relaxed and comfortable.

Arrange chairs into groups of two (see diagram above right). Counseling materials such as *Personal Commitment Guides* and pencils should be placed for use at each pair of chairs. Having these materials on clipboards will make them more convenient for the decision counselors. Have extra chairs nearby for use when a decision counselor will be talking with a couple who have made a decision or when parents sit in with a child being counseled.

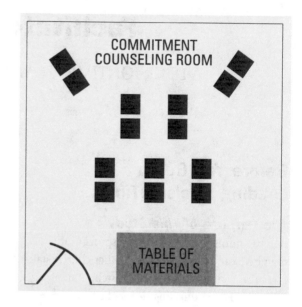

Set up a table near the entrance to the room. Use this table to display follow-up resources for decision makers as well as extra Bibles, pencils, *Personal Commitment Guides*, boxes of tissue, and other items your church decides to use.

Schedule

DecisionTime is a seven-session, small-group study. It is best to meet every week for seven consecutive weeks. After the introductory session, participants will complete a weekly unit of the member's workbook each day for five days in preparation for the next group session. The group sessions should be about one hour. However, you may decide to increase that time. The sessions are designed to overview and offer group experiences that provide a more tangible understanding of commitment counseling.

As facilitator, you will guide the participants as they learn, apply, and evaluate the previous week's material. Your job is not to teach the material to the group members. The workbook is self-instructional, and you do not need to repeat everything the participants have already learned from working through the material.

Use this facilitator's guide to lead the weekly group study. You may decide to expand the number of sessions such as inviting a children's leaders to lead a session specifically on counseling children who make decisions.

Each of the six units is divided into five days of study to be completed at home in 15-20 minutes per day. As study group members read and complete the workbook, they will study the biblical basis for decisions and develop skills for decision counseling.

Enlistment

The pastor and coordinator need to enlist decision counselors for this training 6-10 weeks before the study begins. Keep in mind that decision counseling is not something to force on anyone. Men and women should feel led by God to pursue this vital ministry.

Using the church newsletter, church bulletin, and/or announcement portions of the worship service have all proved to be effective ways of information the congregation about training for such a ministry. However, a personal invitation is still the most effective means to enlist members. Identify those in the church you feel God might lead into this ministry. Call or visit each of those persons to present the opportunity to serve God in this way.

Offer this course once or twice a year. This will give you a broad base of decision counselors.

Room and Equipment

Choose a room for the weekly sessions that is large enough to accommodate members in practice groups. Arrange the chairs in a semicircle. The environment for this study should be friendly and comfortable. Consider have Christian music playing as participants arrive for each session.

Prepare separate display tables of some of the follow-up resources for decision makers (page 100) and for commitment counselors (page 101).

For the weekly sessions, arrange to have a dry-erase board and dry-erase markers or a flip chart and markers or a chalkboard and chalk.

If some of the participants will not know each other, make name tags.

Order of Worship Service

The decision counseling process usually takes 5-15 minutes. Some churches have chosen to rearrange their order of worship to move the offering and announcements following the invitation. That may enable some of those being counseled to be presented before the end of the service. However, the decision counselors should not feel rushed. The decision maker can be presented in a later service.

Note to Decision Makers

A note similar to the following could be printed on a card for the pew rack or could be placed in the worship bulletin. This would let visitors as well as church members know about decisions that could be made during the service and about the commitment counseling process.

Our Invitation to You

We are praying that God will speak to you in a personal way during this worship experience. As He speaks, you may become aware of the need to make some personal commitment to Him. Near the end of the service, you will be invited to come to the front of the worship center. At this time, one of our trained commitment counselors will be happy to assist you in any of the following ways:

• To make a first-time commitment to Jesus,
• To follow Jesus in scriptural baptism,
• To become a member of this church,
• To receive assurance of your salvation,
• To rededicate yourself to grow toward spiritual maturity,
• To make a commitment to a vocational Christian ministry,
• To pray with you concerning some other spiritual need.

We trust that God will meet the most significant need in your life today. May we share with you and rejoice as He works out His will in your life?

Praying for you,

_____, Pastor

Follow-up

The decision counseling experience is crucial. However, follow-up visits, phone calls, and correspondence are essential. Especially important is a visit from someone from the decision maker's Sunday School class or department (or the one he or she would be in if not already enrolled). Other important visits are from the pastor, other church staff, and/or a deacon.

Consider using some of the follow-up resources for decision makers described on page 100.

Materials

Obtain an ample supply of *Personal Commitment Guides.* You will need at least one for each person expected for the training. You will also need enough for those making decisions over the next several months. Order the *Personal Commitment Guides* by calling 1-800-458-2772, faxing 1-615-251-5933, or by writing LifeWay Church Resources Customer Service Center; One LifeWay Plaza; Nashville, TN 37234-00113.

Order enough of these *DecisionTime: Commitment Counseling* workbooks to distribute during the introductory group session. Order the *DecisionTime* workbooks by calling 1-800-458-2772, faxing 1-615-251-5933, or by writing LifeWay Church Resources Customer Service Center; One LifeWay Plaza; Nashville, TN 37234-0113.

Leading Session 1 Introduction

Before This Session

• Complete all six weeks of the *DecisionTime* workbook before the first session so you will know the big picture of this study. Then, you will review each week's study before each of the other sessions.
• Invite the pastor or another church staff member to participate in this session to emphasize the importance of the decision counseling ministry, to clarify any unique aspects of the ministry for your church, and to encourage those being trained.

- Review "During This Session" below.
- Prepare any teaching aids you wish to add.
- Have copies of the *DecisionTime* workbook and the *Personal Commitment Guide* ready to distribute to each participant.
- Prepare a display of the follow-up resources for decision makers (p. 100) and commitment counselors (p. 101).
- If needed, have name tags ready.

During This Session

- As you open the session, take a moment to make certain that everyone knows all the other members of the group. Use name tags if needed.
- Ask each participant to share briefly why he or she decided to participate in this training.
- Read Matthew 28:18-20. Comment that this ministry is one way to participate in fulfilling The Great Commission.
- Introduce the pastor or another church staff member who will pray and then emphasize the importance of the decision counseling ministry, clarify any unique aspects of the ministry for your church, and encourage those being trained. Allow about 20-30 minutes for this presentation followed by a time for questions.
- Distribute a *Decision Time: Commitment Counseling workbook* to each participant. Briefly review the table of contents. State that the following group sessions will provide an opportunity to discuss and practice what they will study during the week.
- Distribute a *Personal Commitment Guide* to each participant. Briefly review the six decisions covered by the *Guide*. Show on page 33 and following that every portion of the *Guide* is shown in the *DecisionTime* workbook alongside the discussion of how to use the *Guide*.

- Ask the group to turn to page 6 and read in unison the five reasons the church needs a group of dedicated and trained decision counselors.
- Assignment: Ask participants to complete Week 1 in the workbook. Show them that this is broken into five daily studies that will take about 15-20 minutes each day.
- Close the session with prayer. Thank God for the willingness of these people to prepare for this significant ministry in the church. Pray for the people in the church and community who will be making decisions and will be helped through this ministry.

Leading Session 2 Commitment Counseling

Before This Session

- Complete Week 1 in this workbook.
- Review "During This Session" below.
- Prepare signs on 8½ by 11 inches paper. Mount these on poster board slightly larger than that. Make holes on each end of the top of the posters. Tie string to each hole. The string should be long enough to fit over a person's head so the sign is on the chest. Make the following signs: Pastor, Coordinator, Trainer, Receiver (make two of these if your church uses more than one receiver), Advisor, Presenter, Decision Counselor (make two or more of these), and Decision Maker (same number as Decision Counselors).
- Prepare any teaching aids you wish to add.
- Prepare the counseling room as it would be set up for a worship service including having the *Personal Commitment Guide* and a pencil on a clip board at each pair of chairs and the display of follow-up resources for decision makers.

During This Session

- Open the session with prayer.
- Give the names of the persons in your church who will be responsible for each function on the decision counseling team. Suggest that they write the name by each function on pages 6-7.

Pastor _____

Coordinator _____

Trainer_____

Receiver_____

Advisor _____

Presenter_____

- Using the signs you have prepared, have different participants represent the functions on the counseling team. You would wear the "Trainer" sign.
- Take the group to the worship center reception area. Using the diagram on page 9, place the "Pastor, " "Receiver(s)," "Coordinator," and "Decision Counselors" in the appropriate location for each function.
- Walk through the process of the "Pastor" extending the invitation for decisions, the "Decision Counselors" coming to their place, the "Decision Makers" coming forward to the "Receiver," the "Receiver" referring the "Decision Maker" to a "Decision Counselor," and the "Coordinator" guiding them to the Commitment Counseling Room.
- Take the group to the decision counseling room. Using the diagram on page 104, place the

"Advisor" and "Decision Counselors" in the appropriate location for each function.
- Walk through the process of the "Decision Maker" sitting with each "Decision Counselor."
- Go back into the worship center and walk through the "Decision Counselor" bringing the "Decision Maker" to the "Presenter" who will present the "Decision Maker" to the congregation. See the diagram on page 9.
- Return to the classroom.
- Direct the participants to point to their mouth; then put their hands to their ears. Say, A good decision counselor listens twice as much (or more) than he or she talks.
- Ask the group to read in unison the paragraph preceding "Barriers to Effective Listening" on page 21 that begins "In order to lead an effective counseling session...."
- Allow participants to discuss what they learned about listening from their study.
- Ask the participants if they have anything else they would like to share from their week's study.
- Assignment: Ask participants to complete Week 2 in the workbook which prepares them to use the double panel on "Salvation" in the *Personal Commitment Guide.* Have them look at the Salvation panel in the *Guide.* Emphasize that this study is the foundation of all commitment counseling sessions. Point out the format that is used in every panel: God's Purpose, Our Need, God's Purpose, Our Response, and My Commitment.
- Ask participants to write on the board or flip chart the names of family members, friends, co-workers, and neighbors who are not Christians. Close the session by praying for these people.

Leading Session 3
Counseling for Salvation

Before This Session

- Complete Week 2 in this workbook.
- Review "During This Session" below.
- Be prepared to lead a simulated decision counseling session on salvation. Enlist one of the participants to be the decision maker. Suggest responses that will demonstrate a fairly typical session with a person ready to receive Jesus as Lord and Savior. Be sure to use all of the Salvation panel and to complete the Commitment Record.
- Have extra copies of the *Personal Commitment Guide* for use in practice in case some of the participants forget to bring theirs with them.
- Prepare any teaching aids you wish to add.
- Continue to have the display of the follow-up resources for decision makers and commitment counselors.

During This Session

- Begin the session with prayer for those who are lost.
- Allow participants to discuss what they learned about salvation from their study.
- Ask the participants if they have anything else they would like to share from their week's study.
- Lead a simulated decision counseling session on salvation with the participant you enlisted to be the decision maker. Use all of the Salvation panel.
- Have the participants work in pairs to practice using all of the Salvation panel. They will take turns being the decision counselor and the decision maker.
- Involve the whole group in a discussion of their experiences during the practice.

- Assignment: Ask participants to complete Week 3 in the workbook which prepares them to use the panels on "Baptism" and "Church Membership" in the *Personal Commitment Guide.*
- Pray for the group participants as they become more comfortable with the decision counseling process.

Leading Session 4
Baptism and Church
Membership

Before This Session

- Complete Week 3 in this workbook.
- Review "During This Session" below.
- Obtain a copy of your church's policy on baptism and church membership. Make enough copies for all participants. If this is not in writing, you could invite the pastor to come to the session to share this.
- Be prepared to lead a simulated decision counseling session on both baptism and church membership. Enlist one of the participants to be the decision maker. Suggest responses that will demonstrate a fairly typical session with a person desiring to be baptized and to become a member of the church. Be sure to start with the Salvation panel to be sure the person has received Jesus as Lord and Savior before moving on to the Baptism and Church Membership panels. Also, complete the Commitment Record.
- Prepare any teaching aids you wish to add.
- Continue to have the display of the follow-up resources for decision makers and commitment counselors.

During This Session

- Begin the session with prayer.
- Distribute and discuss your church's policy on baptism and church membership.
- Allow participants to discuss what they learned about baptism and church membership from their study.
- Ask the participants if they have anything else they would like to share from their week's study.
- Lead a simulated decision counseling session on both baptism and church membership with the participant you enlisted to be the decision maker. Start with the Salvation panel, then move to the Baptism and Church Membership panels. Also, demonstrate completing the Commitment Record.
- Have the participants work in pairs to practice using the Baptism and Church Membership panels. They will take turns being the decision counselor and the decision maker.
- Involve the whole group in a discussion of their experiences during the practice.
- Assignment: Ask participants to complete Week 4 in the workbook which prepares them to use the panel on "Assurance of Salvation" in the *Personal Commitment Guide.*
- Pray for those who will be coming to make decisions in your church.

Leading Session 5 Assurance of Salvation

Before This Session

- Complete Week 4 in this workbook.
- Review "During This Session" below.
- Be prepared to lead a simulated decision counseling session on assurance of salvation. Enlist one of the participants to be the decision maker. Suggest responses that will demonstrate a fairly

typical session with a person who is having doubts. Be sure to start with the Salvation panel to be sure the person has received Jesus as Lord and Savior before moving to the Assurance of Salvation panel. Also, complete the Commitment Record.
- Prepare any teaching aids you wish to add.
- Continue to have the display of the follow-up resources for decision makers and commitment counselors.

During This Session

- Begin the session with prayer.
- Allow participants to discuss what they learned about assurance of salvation from their study.
- Ask the participants if they have anything else they would like to share from their week's study.
- Lead a simulated decision counseling session on assurance of salvation with the participant you enlisted to be the decision maker. Start with the Salvation panel, then move to the Assurance of Salvation panel. Also, demonstrate completing the Commitment Record.
- Have the participants work in pairs to practice using the Assurance of Salvation panel. They will take turns being the decision counselor and the decision maker.
- Involve the whole group in a discussion of their experiences during the practice.
- Assignment: Ask participants to complete Week 5 in the workbook which prepares them to use the panel on "Rededication to Grow Toward Spiritual Maturity" in the *Personal Commitment Guide.*
- Pray for those who need assurance of their salvation.

Leading Session 6 Rededication to Grow Toward Spiritual Maturity

Before This Session
- Complete Week 5 in this workbook.
- Review "During This Session" below.
- Be prepared to lead a simulated decision counseling session on rededication to grow toward spiritual maturity. Enlist one of the participants to be the decision maker. Suggest responses that will demonstrate a fairly typical session with a person who is convicted by the Holy Spirit concerning this need to grow. Be sure to start with the Salvation panel to be sure the person has received Jesus as Lord and Savior before moving to the Rededication panel. Also, demonstrate completion of the Commitment Record.
- Prepare any teaching aids you wish to add.
- Continue to have the display of the follow-up resources for decision makers and commitment counselors.

During This Session
- Begin the session with prayer.
- Allow participants to discuss what they learned about rededication to grow toward spiritual maturity from their study.
- Ask the participants if they have anything else they would like to share from their week's study.
- Lead a simulated decision counseling session on rededication to grow toward spiritual maturity with the participant you enlisted to be the decision maker. Start with the Salvation panel, then move to the Rededication to Grow Toward Spiritual Maturity panel. Also, demonstrate completing the Commitment Record.

- Have the participants work in pairs to practice using the Rededication to Grow Toward Spiritual Maturity panel. They will take turns being the decision counselor and the decision maker.
- Involve the whole group in a discussion of their experiences during the practice.
- Assignment: Ask participants to complete Week 6 in the workbook which prepares them to use the panel on "Commitment to Vocational Christian Ministry" in the *Personal Commitment Guide* and for other distinct decision counseling situations.
- Pray for those in your church who will be convicted by the Holy Spirit concerning a need to grow spiritually.

Leading Session 7 Distinct Counseling Situations

Before This Session
- Complete Week 6 in this workbook.
- Review "During This Session" below.
- Be prepared to lead a simulated decision counseling session with a child coming for salvation. Enlist one of the participants to be the child. Suggest responses that will demonstrate a fairly typical session with a child. You might prefer to ask a children's leader to provide this demonstration.
- Prepare any teaching aids you wish to add.
- Continue to have the display of the follow-up resources for decision makers and commitment counselors.

During This Session

- Begin the session with prayer.
- Allow participants to discuss what they learned about distinctive counseling situations from this week's study.
- Ask the participants if they have anything else they would like to share from the week's study.
- Lead a simulated decision counseling session with a child coming for salvation with the participant you enlisted to be the child. Or, introduce the children's leader you enlisted to provide this demonstration.
- Have the participants work in pairs. Have one of the pair to practice being a decision maker counseling a child using the Salvation panel. Then, the other person will practice being the decision counselor using the Commitment to Vocational Christian Ministry panel.
- Involve the whole group in a discussion of their experiences during the practice.
- Review the follow-up resources for commitment counselors on page 101.
- Invite persons who have studied each of the resources to share how that particular study would prepare them further for ministry as decision counselors.
- Allow time for every group member to pray for this ministry. Then close the prayer time.